DAYS of "UNCERTAINTY AND DREAD"

THE ORDEAL ENDURED
BY THE CITIZENS AT GETTYSBURG

By Gerald R. Bennett

Gerald R. Bennett

9/13/'14

II

Published and Distributed by the Gettysburg Foundation
1195 Baltimore Pike, Gettysburg, PA 17325
www.gettysburgfoundation.org
717-334-1243

Printed by Huggins Printing Company
2900 Sycamore Street, Harrisburg, PA 17111

1st Printing, 1994
2nd Printing, 1996
3rd Printing, 1997
4th Printing, 2002
5th Printing, 2008
Revised 1997
Revised 2002
Revised 2008

ISBN 0-9643599-3-6

TABLE OF CONTENTS

LIST OF PHOTOGRAPHS AND ABBREVIATIONS

ABBREVIATIONS;
ACHS = The Adams County Historical Society
GNMP = Gettysburg National Military Park
GRB =Gerald R. Bennett
USMHI = United States Military History Institute

ACKNOWLEDGMENTS

It goes without exception that any finished work such as this one is not the sole output of the author. Many persons touch the project at various times in ways that materially aid in shaping the final product. I will attempt to recognize all with full knowledge that I will probably unintentionally omit someone deserving of mention. For this, I apologize.

First are those 1863 citizens of Gettysburg who took the time to record their experiences and memories of those tumultuous days that impacted their lives so long ago. If they had not done so, there would be no story to write or read.

My deepest gratitude goes to the tireless staff at the Adams County Historical Society. Their cheerful and constant assistance, in guiding me to the source data housed in the Society's remarkable archives, literally made it possible for me to transform my dream into a reality. I thank Dr. Charles Glatfelter, Elwood Christ and Tim Smith for their generous support, help and encouragement.

The generosity of Don Troiani, in my humble opinion the Rembrandt among historical artists, likewise commands my deepest gratitude for permitting the use of his dramatic rendition of Gettysburg civilians seeking shelter in their cellar as my cover centerpiece.

My thanks go to Fred and Nancy Edmunds, two dear friends, for their encouragement and helpful suggestions. It was Fred who recommended the front cover design.

Harry W. Pfanz, noted historian and author of three monumental books on Gettysburg's first and second day battles, generously read a preliminary version of the manuscript. He offered a number of insightful comments which aided significantly in refining the final product.

I'm sure many authors, as I did, reach a point during their work when they come to doubt the quality and worth of their labors. That moment for me came at the completion of the manuscript. It was my family, my wife Ellie and children Mike, Laurie and Robin, who got me beyond that hurdle. Each agreed to read a manuscript on a subject about which they had no prior interest or knowledge and found themselves engrossed in the story. Their individual and collective feedback served to convince me to go ahead and publish this book.

Thank you, one and all.

FORWARD

This is a story about people, the citizens of Gettysburg, Pennsylvania, in the summer of 1863. While these people lived over 145 years ago, the traumatic events and emotional experiences they endured during the days of June and July 1863 can readily be transferred to our present day consciousness. This is because their story is narrated in their own words. Words, whose meaning and impact convey understanding for all generations.

Fortunately a significant number of people who lived through those tumultuous days left the future generations with their vivid and sensitive, personal accounts. Undoubtedly many others did the same in private correspondence that has been lost over time. The recollections that remain are more than adequate to reconstruct the incredible story of human resourcefulness, courage and endurance demonstrated by the citizens at Gettysburg, when two huge armies engulfed their town in violent warfare.

This book is not about the fighting that took place at Gettysburg. It is about the physical and emotional impact the armies and their epic struggle had on the town and its citizens. It is about the inner strength and resiliency the citizens brought forth to persevere and triumph over adversity of unimaginable proportions.

Their story begins with their earliest fears for safety in the initial weeks following the outbreak of the Civil War. It continues as the townspeople struggle to deal with the rising apprehension generated by the growing realization that the "Rebels Are Coming," during the three weeks of June preceding the actual arrival of the opposing armies. It chronicles the events of 2 1/2 days of Confederate occupation and how the strain of living under martial law brings out the best, and in a few cases the worst, in the entrapped citizenry. When the tide of battle recedes, the town and its population must face a new invasion and a new set of overwhelming challenges; the 21,000 wounded left behind, the shortage of food, the cleaning up of the debris of battle, and the sudden arrival of hordes of visitors from around the country. Their story continues, and once more the citizens of Gettysburg prove to be uncommonly resilient, as they meet and overcome these new adversities. Their story ends with a final event, one which yet again tests the town's modest resources and the population's determination and ability to cope. For a third time in six months thousands flock to Gettysburg. This time the occasion is to celebrate the dedication of the Soldiers National Cemetery and the rebirth of the nation, as defined by President Lincoln in his Gettysburg Address. As on the two prior occasions, the town and its people survive the ordeal. Unlike the earlier events, this time the citizens willingly participate and rejoice in the proceedings.

The individuals who left memoirs generally chronicled affairs as they saw them in their immediate neighborhood. I was fortunate to find reminiscences by persons living in various sections of the town. As a result I have been able to reconstruct a fairly even representation of how the town was impacted and how people reacted. Having made that point, I must concede the fact that the majority of accounts were concentrated in the center area of town. This provides an imbalance of first hand coverage to a few prominent areas such as High, Middle, Chambersburg and Baltimore streets. The reader should not misinterpret this fact to mean that these were the only areas in town that participated in or suffered from the trying events brought about by the battle at Gettysburg. The ordeal was common to everyone and everywhere in the town.

One final clarification on the scope of the subject for this book. I have presented the story of the events and experiences that befell those who resided in the Borough of Gettysburg. There are a number of fascinating memoirs of civilians who lived just beyond the Borough limits and out in the countryside. They have been purposely omitted in keeping with the objective of this narrative. Additionally, a number of interesting events, involving only soldiers and their combat experiences within the town, were likewise omitted.

With no further caveats, I hope you, the reader, find the story of the citizens' life at Gettysburg in the summer and fall of 1863 as fascinating as I have.

> Gerald R. Bennett
> Gettysburg, Pa.
> July 18, 1994

P.S. At this the 5th printing I have again taken the liberty to make some minor revisions. This is because on-going research has exposed additional civilian accounts which I believe enrich the story of Gettysburg's unique experience. I have also corrected some minor errors which also came to light due to further study.

GRB
7/30/2008

MAP KEYS

Map A: Gettysburg Borough

1. Sarah Broadhead
2. The Eagle Hotel
3. Dr. Robt. & Mary Horner
4. Mary McAllister
5. Charles McCurdy
6. Leander Warren
7. John Will/Globe Inn
8. David Wills
9. Sarah King
10. Liberty Hollinger
11. Prof. Martin Stoever/
    J. L. Schick's Store
12. Moses McClean family
13. William McClean
14. Gates Fahnestock
15. Fahnestock Bros. Store
16. Daniel Skelly
17. Michael Jacobs family
18. Mary Warren
19. David Kendlehart
20. Fannie Buehler
21. Salome Myers
22. Alice Powers
23. Catherine Foster
24. Albertus McCreary
25. Agnes Barr
26. Mary & Jennie Wade
27. Tillie Pierce
28. Catherine & Anna Garlach
29. Winebrenner/M. L. Culler
30. Harvey Sweney
31. Samuel McCreary
32. Henry Rupp
33. Georgia Wade McClellan/
    Jennie Wade killed
34. Cemetery Gatehouse (Thorn)
35. Nellie Aughinbaugh
36. John Burns
37. Anthony Sellinger

A. Christ Lutheran Church
B. The McClellan House
C. St. James Lutheran Church
D. Methodist Church
E. Adams County Courthouse
F. German Reformed Church
G. Gettysburg Public School
H. Catholic Church
I. Presbyterian Church
J. United Presbyterian Church
K. Eyster's Female Academy
L. Gettysburg R.R. station
M. Pennsylvania College
N. to Oak Ridge Seminary
O. to Lutheran Seminary
P. The Wagon Hotel
Q. Cemetery Hill
W. Warehouses

Map B: Gettysburg and Vicinity

1. Pennsylvania College
2. Carrie Sheads' Oak Ridge Seminary
3. Lutheran Seminary

X

Map A:
Gettysburg
Borough

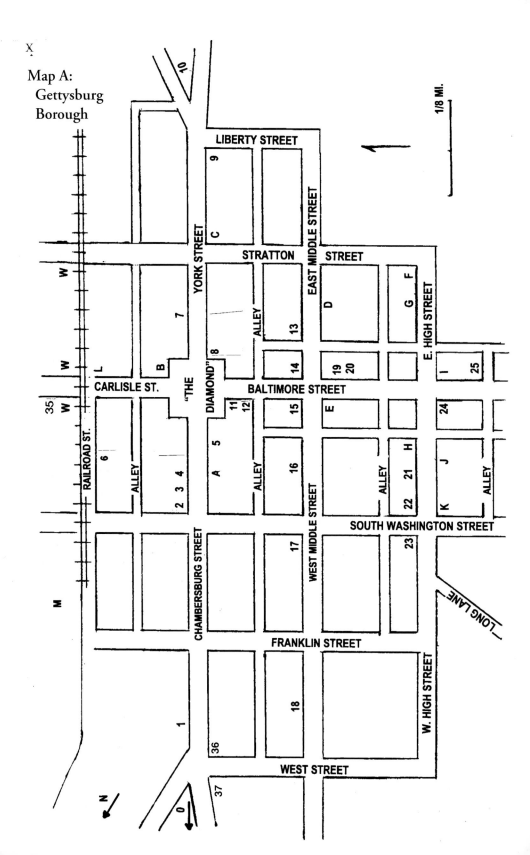

Map A:
Gettysburg
Borough

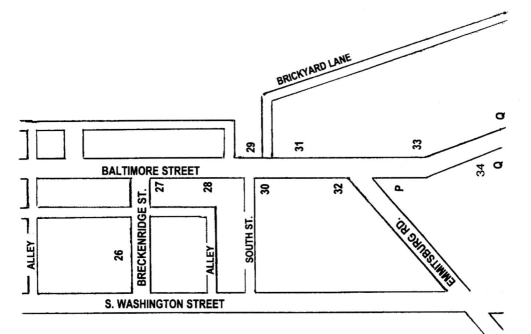

BRICKYARD LANE

Q

29   31   33

34 Q

BALTIMORE STREET

27   28

30   32   P

SOUTH ST.

BRECKENRIDGE ST.

ALLEY

26

ALLEY

EMMITSBURG RD.

S. WASHINGTON STREET

1/8 MI.

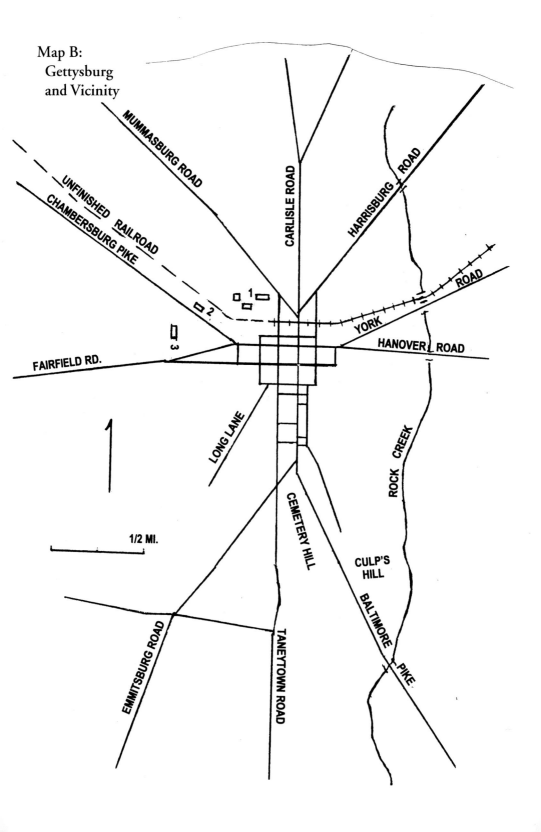

Map B:
Gettysburg
and Vicinity

MUMMASBURG ROAD

UNFINISHED RAILROAD

CHAMBERSBURG PIKE

CARLISLE ROAD

HARRISBURG ROAD

ROAD

YORK

1

2

3

FAIRFIELD RD.

HANOVER ROAD

LONG LANE

ROCK CREEK

1/2 MI.

CEMETERY HILL

CULP'S
HILL

BALTIMORE PIKE

EMMITSBURG ROAD

TANEYTOWN ROAD

INTRODUCTION:

"Every hour was one of uncertainty and dread," is how one Gettysburg resident remembered those first three days of July, 1863.[1]   The editor of the ADAMS SENTINEL was a bit more expansive in his view of what the town and its civilian population had just experienced. Using phraseology usually reserved for the pulpit, he reviewed the events of the preceding week: "Remembering that our town was the dividing line between two opposing forces...We can do nothing less than gratefully and reverently acknowledge the Divine favor which has watched over our lives and our homes."[2]

The event was one that few Americans, in the course of our long history, have had to endure; war in our town, in our streets, in our yards and in our houses. Books, articles and reminiscences, too numerous to count, have chronicled the clashes of the armies on the fields surrounding Gettysburg. Comparative little has been written about what happened in the town of Gettysburg and to the people who lived there.

Historians of the battle usually gloss over the fact that Gettysburg, with its nearly 450 buildings, its 2400 inhabitants, its economic and social structures, was in the midst of the fighting during those terrible three days.[3]   Men fought and died in the streets. For two and a half days the town was occupied by a hostile army and subjected to the dangers of the deadly missiles of war. The town and its citizens were still there when the armies departed, leaving behind them the damage and flotsam of battle and 21,000 helpless wounded needing care.[4]   The story of what this village community had to endure, and the human resourcefulness and resilience displayed in dealing with the titanic events before, during and following the battle days of July 1-3, 1863, is heroic.

In order for this story to be fully appreciated it is helpful to be acquainted with some of the demographics of the town. Founded in 1786, Gettysburg was far from just another sleepy, little, rural village. While the surrounding countryside consisted of small crop farms, Gettysburg had an unusually diversified cultural structure. Foremost, it served as the seat of government for Adams County. There were the numerous attorneys associated with the activities of county court business. There were the usual merchants and banks necessary to support the needs of the town and surrounding farm families. There was industrial commerce. Tradesmen worked as independent 'cottage industries' rather than in factories so common in the New England towns.

The leading industries were carriage manufacturing and blacksmithing. There were four tanneries, but no shoe factory. An examination of the 1860 Census for Gettysburg does reveal more people engaged in making and/or selling shoes (thirty) than normally would be expected to meet the demand of the town's modest population, but no vast shoe supply was available for needy Confederate troops. Legend to the contrary, the facts do not support the lure of Gettysburg's shoes to Lee's army as the cause for the combatants to unexpectedly meet there.

Gettysburg was a center for higher education, hosting Pennsylvania College (now Gettysburg College) and a Lutheran Seminary. The students and faculty of these two institutions added a layer of erudition among the population not usually found in rural villages.

Gettysburg was also something of a transportation center. The town developed around a key cross road that linked central Pennsylvania with Baltimore and Washington to the south and Philadelphia and Pittsburgh to the east and west. By 1863 no less than ten major roads merged in Gettysburg from various points on the compass. In 1858 the railroad arrived, linking the town via the most advanced transportation technology with the major cities to the north, east and south, as far as Baltimore and Washington. In support of the commerce generated by these transportation facilities, hotels flourished. This relatively small town had no less than six hotel/tavern establishments.

Communications was an important element in the town's culture. The townspeople's cosmopolitan interests and intellectual curiosity, coupled with strong political allegiances, supported three weekly newspapers; THE COMPILER, the voice of the Democrats, and it's Republican counterparts, THE STAR and BANNER and THE ADAMS SENTINEL. The political bias used to interpret news events was obviously important to the local readership. The source material for national news was borrowed mainly from the pages of Washington and Baltimore newspapers. The newspapers and the telegraph office, which arrived in December 1862, kept Gettysburg in touch with what was going on in the rest of the country.

It would be a gross inaccuracy to assume that the citizens of this small town were blissfully homogenous. Partisan political philosophies were the basis for strong opposing opinions among Gettysburg citizens. The division of allegiance between Democrats and Republicans was fairly even, with the edge in local voting belonging to the former, even though Abraham Lincoln carried the county by a razor thin margin in the presidential election of 1860.[5] On the issue of slavery, the overwhelming sentiment was against the institution, but not necessarily pro abolitionism. The town like the county was strongly pro Union, but the 'Confederate Cause' was not without it's sympathizers. Some individuals in town were considered "Copperheads."[6] For a few, rancorous emotions grew out of differing political philosophies.

Unfortunately this bitterness would manifest itself during those stressful days in 1863 in some bizarre incidents of citizen turning upon citizen.

Strong religious convictions were deeply instilled within the citizenship and denominations were as diverse as the social and economic makeup of the general population. There were seven churches in the town. The collective faith of the Gettysburg citizens in the Righteousness of the Almighty would prove to be a major factor in their individual ability to cope and survive what befell them in the summer of 1863.

Physically, the town was constructed in much the same manner as the large, eastern cities. The layout was symmetrical along an east-west and north-south street plan extending from a central square, locally called the 'Diamond.' There were very few front yards. The buildings, the vast majority of brick construction, generally fronted the edge of the brick sidewalks or pavements as they were known.

The streets were broad and unpaved. Almost all the building lots in the first two blocks radiating east, west and south from the 'Diamond' were developed. This presented an unbroken frontage of houses and shops that restricted movement through the town to the streets and alleys. Many of the back yards were surrounded by high board fences, further impeding free movement. The difficulty in readily moving large bodies of troops through the town proved to be a significant factor during the battle. The most dramatic impact came about when the Union forces attempted to withdraw southward through the town to Cemetery Hill on the afternoon of the first day's fight. The congestion in the streets and alleys served to entrap a significant number of the fleeing soldiers and led to their capture, and, in some instances, to their death.

Besides being fenced, the back yards were highly functional in the fabric of town life. The lots were deep and contained the usual stable/carriage house, a well, the "privy" and the essential kitchen garden. The latter trio of these facilities would be completely overwhelmed by the demands of the Confederate occupation and the influx of visitors immediately following the departure of the two armies.

Gettysburg was a prosperous, fully developed and vibrant town that found itself perched in the path of harms way beginning in the middle days of June, 1863. Nothing in their collective experiences could have prepared them to anticipate and meet the level of adversity they would be forced to endure that summer. The enormity of the impact thrust upon their being and on the structure of their community by the sudden arrival of 163,000 men and 15,000 thousand animals, involved in the most violent form of activity, was simply unimaginable.

JUNE 15TH - 30TH:
"Unmistakable signs..began to accumulate"

The Rebels are coming! By June 1863 this was a cry familiar to the residents in and around Gettysburg. The war was barely one week old when they encountered their first experience with that dreaded alarm. Early on the morning of June 22, 1861, citizens gathered at the railroad station to send the 'GETTYSBURG BLUES', the local and mainly ceremonial militia infantry company, off to the war. The departure of the 'Blues' made many feel uneasy about the security of the community; a feeling intensified by the fact that Maryland and Baltimore, with openly pro Southern sympathies, were nearby neighbors, and Confederate Virginia almost as close.

That same evening a town meeting was held in the courthouse to propose raising a Home Guard to provide protection and to relieve apprehensions about safety for the town. The business at hand was rudely and unexpectedly interrupted by two strangers bursting into the packed courtroom with the news: "The Rebels are burning Hanover and Gettysburg is next!" It was reported that over "500 Rebel pug-uglies" from Baltimore were heading to Gettysburg. Almost before the crowd had time to react, a single horseman entered town along York Street, shouting the alarm, "To arms. The Rebels are coming!"[1] It was more than the collective psyche of the citizenry could handle. Calm gave way to pandemonium. Everyone poured into the streets. The news spread through the town like wildfire. Bells tolled the alarm. Riders were dispatched to warn neighboring hamlets of the danger. All arms (except fowling pieces) and ammunition had departed earlier that day with the 'BLUES,' "..adding a hundredfold to the excitement."[2] The streets were a scene of the wildest confusion. The town was doing its best to prepare for a siege with axes and garden hoes substituting for rifles. The night held no promise or concern for sleep. Sometime after midnight cooler heads did prevail and a locomotive was fired up and sent east toward Hanover to reconnoiter the situation. In the interim, while awaiting the news from the locomotive and crew, one can imagine the almost comical spectacle of a squad of determined citizens, armed with a few shotguns and garden implements, patrolling the town streets. Shortly before dawn the engine returned with the news that the alarm was false and the Rebel mob non-existent. Calm returned as quickly as it had disappeared.[3] The unknown alarmists, whose bogus news had touched off the fracas, were long gone from the scene.

This would be the first of many alarms about impending attack from imaginary Rebels. As the war ground along, amateur scouts patrolled the roads in the countryside that led to the Potomac River. On several occasions these scouts came dashing into town shouting, "The Rebels are coming."[4] These incidents resulted in a wild scurry by persons owning prized horses or live stock to move their animals to places of safety. More than once, bank officers packed up their currency and sent it to Philadelphia for safe keeping. Merchants likewise took precautions and prepared their most valuable goods for rapid evacuation.[5]

On other occasions Gettysburg received the news of raiding Rebels in a secondary manner. An alarm of invading Confederates in the counties to the west would send caravans of refugees passing through Gettysburg, heading to safer places across the Susquehanna River. John Will, living at the Globe Inn in the first block of York Street, remembered a typical scene: "..it was a sight at night in the moonlight to see them going through town with loaded wagons, the majority going eastward..to places of safety." With few exceptions the reported Confederate raiders, triggering these panic driven flights, proved to be nonexistent.[6]

Those psychologically impacted the hardest by these alarms of approaching Rebels were the members of Gettysburg's free, black community. There were over 150 living in the town, some of whom had begun their lives as slaves.[7] Their fear of bodily harm, or capture and forced impoundment into the dreaded institution by the Confederates, was cause enough for them to flee their homes whenever the cry, "the Rebels are coming," was heralded on the streets. Tillie Pierce, a school girl living on the corner of Baltimore and Breckenridge Streets, remembered some years later that whenever the alarm came, the black citizens would flee from their homes in the southwest part of town, down Breckenridge St., and on toward Culp's Hill to secret hideouts. Tillie described the scene: "I can see them yet; men and women with bundles...slung across their backs, almost bearing them to the ground. Children also carrying their bundles, striving in vain to keep up with their seniors. The greatest consternation was depicted on all of their countenances..." Anxious mothers would stop to hurry the children, warning them of a terrible fate if they lagged behind and were caught by the rebels.[8] For these folks the suffering was real, even if the reports of raiding Confederates were false.

There was one occasion, before the Confederate invasion of Pennsylvania in 1863, when the alarm, "the rebels are coming," was real. In October of 1862, Lee's cavalry chief, Jeb Stuart, crossed the Potomac with his troopers on a raid into southern Pennsylvania. Moving northeast along the Cumberland Valley he entered Chambersburg. Turning east along present day U.S. Rte. 30 he headed directly towards Gettysburg. On October 11th he reached Cashtown, 8 miles to the west. Here he turned south toward Fairfield taking horses, provisions and seven hostages. His scouts were reported as close as Latshaw's Tavern, just six miles from Gettysburg, setting off yet another alarm and panic in the town.[9] Calm was quickly restored when pursuing Federal troops arrived on the 12th and stayed overnight. Stuart made good his escape to the south and the Potomac River. The friendly troops left and the excitement quickly passed away.[10]

It is difficult for anyone not experiencing these events to evaluate the impact that they had on the collective psyche of the Gettysburg community by the early summer of 1863. A study of citizen reminiscences about those tumultuous days of June and July suggests that most underestimated the potential of real danger. Perhaps there was an element of the "cry wolf" syndrome. Or perhaps it was just wishful thinking, comfort gained in hoping that this too would just go away. It is impossible for us to say. Whatever the cause, a sizable portion of the population appeared to have been genuinely surprised when Lee's army really came and the great battle happened.[11]

There was no tangible reason for anyone in Gettysburg to underestimate the coming menace. It was clear to at least one resident. Professor Michael Jacobs was emphatic about the evidence of impending danger when writing his memoirs about those days shortly after the battle ended: "Unmistakable signs of the coming storm began to accumulate."[12]

Within days after Lee started his infantry columns from Fredericksburg toward the Shenandoah Valley, Federal authorities began to suspect his objective to be an invasion of Maryland and possibly southern Pennsylvania. On June 11th the War Department appointed Major General Darius N. Couch to head up the newly created Department of the Susquehanna with headquarters located at Harrisburg. Gov. Andrew Curtin of Pennsylvania was certainly not in the dark as to the growing danger. On June 12th he issued a statewide proclamation, in concert with a plea from General Couch, urging citizens to organize and hasten to the defense of the Commonwealth. That message was probably received in Gettysburg on the following day.

Meanwhile Lee's army was moving rapidly northward. On June 13th, they fell on the Union garrison at Winchester, Va. driving out the defenders while inflicting heavy casualties. One of those receiving a mortal wound was Johnston Skelly Jr. of the 87th Pa., a native and citizen of Gettysburg. His good friend (perhaps fiancé?) and pen-pal, Jennie Wade, would suffer the same fate in Gettysburg less than three weeks later.

Early on June 15th, Jenkin's Confederate cavalry brigade crossed the Potomac, passed quickly through Hagerstown, Maryland and reached Chambersburg Pennsylvania before nightfall. Chambersburg is just 25 miles west of Gettysburg. Confederate patrols moved out into the surrounding country side confiscating horses and other provisions. This triggered the usual refugee migration to the east. Gettysburg would soon hear the all too familiar alarm, "the Rebels are coming."

There were others, besides Professor Jacobs, whose recollections indicate that Gettysburg was by no means in the dark about the events pointing to a real Confederate invasion. Sarah Broadhead who kept a thorough diary of those days, noted in her entry for June 15th: "Today we heard that the Rebels were crossing the river (Potomac) in heavy force and advancing on this state." No alarm was felt until Gov. Curtain telegraphed a warning directing people to move their stores.[13]

Gettysburg was finally moved to action as the rumors of the rebel advance poured into town. Merchants, like the Fahnestock Brothers and John L. Schick, loaded up the standby rail cars they had leased with their best merchandise and sent them to Philadelphia for safe keeping. Bank funds were sent away. Private citizens, at least the wealthier ones, arranged for space on these cars and sent their most cherished valuables and papers along. Prized carriage and riding horses were sent to distant places, where it was expected they would be out of harms way.[14]

Amidst all of this frantic activity, the familiar anxieties returned to the local population. Salome Myers, a 21 year old school teacher living in the first block of W. High St., recalled: "The people did little more than stand along the street and talk. Whenever someone heard a new report all flocked to him. The suspense was dreadful...there was no social life in town at the time."[15]

In the early hours of June 16th anxiety escalated into momentary panic. Around 1 A.M. the sky to the southwest began to glow with the reflection of flames from a huge fire. The excited shouts from people in the streets of town announced, "the Rebels are coming and burning as they go." Fannie Buehler remembered that the townspeople were: "..in a condition to believe anything. The whole town was in the streets all night long discussing the possibilities."[16] In a few hours the facts of the situation were made known and the panic and excitement abated. The streets cleared as tired and weary citizens returned to their beds for the few hours left before the dawn of a new day arrived. The fire was one that broke out in Emmitsburg Maryland, 12 miles to the south-east, and consumed 27 buildings in the heart of the town. It was started by an act of arson, but the Confederates had no hand in that event. The rest of June 16 passed quietly and tense nerves began to relax.

The next day the emotional pendulum quickly reversed when once again the sudden alarm that the "Rebels Are Coming!" swept through the town. Salome Myers noted the mood swing in her diary: "The town was in a perfect uproar. The excitement was intense for awhile, but it gradually subsided when it [the alarm] was found to be false."[17]

The Rebels had not appeared and the citizens began to believe that it was just a repeat of a familiar cycle. Fannie Buehler recalled: "When they did not come, we lost faith in their coming and it grew to be an old story. We tried to make ourselves believe that they would never come."[18] Here was a open admission that some people were turning to denial to help deal with their extreme stress and anxiety. This was an understandable, but dangerous thought process in light of the real circumstances beginning to engulf them. This time something was different.

Reports of a Confederate threat persisted and preparations in Gettysburg to meet that threat moved ahead. On June 17th a crowd gathered in front of Alexander Buehler's Drug Store in the first block of Chambersburg Street. There a group of 83 men, including 61 students from the college and seminary, had assembled to respond to Gov. Curtin's call for volunteers to throw out the Rebels.[19] After signing up, the town's newest soldiers immediately embarked for Harrisburg. On the 19th they arrived at Camp Curtin in the state capitol and mustered-in as Company A, 26th PA. Emergency Volunteer (P.E.V.) Infantry.

On this same day, June 19th, Major Granville O. Haller from General Couch's staff arrived in Gettysburg to address the town on the status of the growing emergency in Pennsylvania and to command local defense forces. The next morning, on June 20th, the courthouse was full as Major Haller urged the townsmen to arm themselves in order to protect their town and state. The reaction to the appeal for the defense of the state was not overly enthusiastic. The townspeople felt that Gettysburg had already done its share by raising Co. A.[20] However, there was sufficient concern for local defense to enable Robert Bell to raise a company of Independent Cavalry. Capt. Bell and his men immediately set about patrolling the roads to the west, looking for signs of Lee's advance.

The following day, June 21st, 40 members of the Philadelphia City Troop rode in from the east to augment Bell's force. This combined company became Gettysburg's sole guardian against the approach of the dreaded Confederate hoards. Their presence was appreciated by the local citizens, but did little to bolster morale which was rapidly eroding under the persistent rumors of the Rebels' approach. Sarah Broadhead's assessment of the protective value of these men was probably reflective of the mood of the whole town when she wrote in her diary: "They can be of little use, since they have never seen service."[21]

Despite their lack of military training Bell's men quickly brought in news of Confederates in the mountains moving east toward Gettysburg. On June 22nd, a group of Gettysburg men, including Sarah Broadhead's husband Joseph, volunteered to try and impede the Rebel advance by felling trees across the roads in the narrow mountain passes. About fifty men started west out the Chambersburg Pike with axes on their shoulders. They soon returned, having encountered the Confederates already on the east side of South Mountain. The startled Rebels fired a few long distance warning shots before both parties turned and quickly retraced their steps to their respective places of origin. Sarah Broadhead noted in her diary that she anticipated sleeping better that night with the knowledge that the Rebels went back across the mountains.[22]

June 23rd passed quietly for Gettysburg. There were no sightings of the Confederates. Excitement picked up again on Wednesday, the 24th. During the comings and goings of Bell's scouts, a telegram from Harrisburg arrived announcing that the 26th P.E.V. would arrive in Gettysburg by rail the next afternoon (June 25th) to intercede in any Confederate attempt to enter the town. Gettysburg undoubtedly reacted to the news with some degree of ambivalence. Once again Sarah Broadhead's diary entry provides an insight as to the town's emotional outlook: "We are getting used to the excitement and many think the enemy...will not favor us with their presence." Optimistic words, yet in the same entry she revealed a pessimistic outlook when referring to the announcement that the 26th P.E.V. regiment would soon be arriving: "We do not feel much safer."[23]

The events of Thursday, June 25th gave a spooky credence to the negative side of the town's emotional equation. Almost as an omen of impending disaster, the 26th P.E.V. was literally sidetracked. Between New Oxford and Gettysburg the train collided with a stray cow and was derailed. None of the soldiers were injured, but their dramatic entry into Gettysburg was postponed until Friday morning, June 26th, when they finally marched into town about 9:00 A.M.[24]

In the meantime, the people in Gettysburg suffered through a very stressful Thursday night. The troops had not arrived and after dark numerous campfires, visible on the eastern slopes of South Mountain where Cashtown is located, signaled the reality that the Rebels were finally coming.

After their belated arrival on Friday morning, the 26th Pa. paused just long enough to receive a gala welcome from the townspeople. That would be the last of their good times. Before noon they moved out Chambersburg Street, with Bell's troopers in the lead, toward Cashtown and a collision with Jubal Early's veteran Confederate infantry. The town was relatively quiet after their departure. Henry Jacobs described it as an "ominous calm." The foundation for this "calm" was very shaky. It probably rested entirely on the general belief, or prayer, that this all would turn out to be a false alarm as it had so many times in the past.[25]

The black community was not so sure, and many of them took the precaution to gather whatever of their possessions that could be carried and headed out of town. Once again they trekked to their familiar hiding places and remained until the crisis passed.[26] One can imagine that this exodus was undertaken with the same emotional stress as their previous ones.

Their precaution was well founded. About 2 P.M. the remnants of Bell's cavalry escort came riding pell-mell down Chambersburg Street with the news that the 26th had been routed and the survivors were in full retreat to the northeast. Furthermore, Confederates not pursuing the 26th were riding on Gettysburg. After sounding the alarm, Bell's men, and those of the Philadelphia City Troop who had stayed behind that morning, spurred their horses into a full gallop and scattered out of town along the roads to the south and east. Gettysburg was left to face it's nightmare alone and defenseless.

The immediate reaction of much of the population was predictable given all that they had been through to date. Sarah Broadhead reported: "No one believed this, for they (Rebels) had so often been reported as coming."[27] When Rebel cavalry appeared reality quickly took hold. Merchants locked their doors and retreated to the second floors of their buildings to peek out from behind shuttered windows. The streets cleared as people everywhere fled to the security of their houses. School children were dismissed and hurried towards home.[28]

The girls attending Carrie Sheads' Oak Ridge Seminary out on the Chambersburg Pike headed back into town at the first warning. On reaching the foot of Chambersburg Street a small group stopped, "..to wait and see if the Rebels were really coming." When the lead Confederate horsemen crested Seminary ridge, a mere half mile away, the children hastily resumed their flight up the street, "..never halting for steps, mud or anything else." When they reached the intersection of Chambersburg and Washington Streets they turned into the lobby of the Eagle Hotel, seeking a safe haven inside the big doors. Despite the gravity of the situation, Owen Hicks was moved to stop his own flight and laugh out loud at the sight of the girls flying madly up the street.[29]

At Rebecca Eyster's Young Ladies Seminary, located at the corner of High and S. Washington Streets, the students were dismissed with a hasty command, "Children, run home as quickly as you can." Tillie Pierce lived just two blocks away and barely reached home before the Confederate horsemen came thundering down Baltimore Street. She was certain,".. some of the girls did not reach their homes before the Rebels were in the streets."[30]

Others, who had reason to fear that they were probable targets for arrest, fled town. Hugh Scott operated the telegraph office located in his parents house in the first block of Chambersburg St. Upon receiving a warning of the Confederates approach from one of Bell's fleeing troopers, he took up his telegraph equipment and headed east to York along the turnpike in a borrowed horse and buggy. The Confederates would later confess their disappointment to a local citizen at not capturing, "..your telegraph apparatus."[31]

David Buehler was another who had to make a hasty retreat. Buehler served as the town's postmaster. When the first word of the Confederate approach reached his house, he and Fannie thought it to be another false alarm. As Fannie recalled: "We...laughed over it." The humor quickly disappeared when David's brother arrived with the news that the Rebs were at the town's outskirts. David rushed outside and proceeded the block and a half to the 'Diamond' to see for himself. What he saw down at the end of Chambersburg Street sent him sprinting back to his home. Fannie met him at the door with a satchel packed with valuable government property and a valise of clothes. Without further ado he left on the run, turning the corner into East Middle Street just as the Rebels started out Baltimore

Street from the square. He made good his escape to Hanover and eventually to his wife's family home in New Jersey. He would not return for almost two weeks. Like many other women whose husbands left to secure valued property, Fannie would face the coming horrors at Gettysburg alone with her children.[32]

A few folks treated the approach of the Confederates as casually as an entertainment event. Upon hearing that the rebels were approaching, 10 year old Charles McCurdy ran down to the foot of Chambersburg street. There he found, "..a crowd of old men and boys looking towards Seminary Ridge." Charles recalled that one boy had a toy cannon made from a piece of gas pipe. To add to the gaiety of the occasion the boy fired a loud salute. Before he could get off a second report, Rebel

Lower end of Chambersburg St. ca 1885. The Chambersburg Pike enters at the left. (ACHS)

horsemen broke over the top of the ridge. The men stopped him from firing again, "..fearing Reb reprisal." With the appearance of the enemy the mood quickly turned somber. It was enough for young Charles: "I waited only for the front line to come into view, making record time for home. . . and stationing myself on the front porch watched the spectacular entry."[33]

The first Confederates to enter Gettysburg were members of White's 35th VA. Battalion of cavalry. As they made the turn into lower Chambersburg St. they spurred into a gallop and headed toward the square, screaming and discharging their weapons into the air. If the intent was to intimidate the townspeople they were only partially successful. Sarah Broadhead was standing in the front door of her house on lower Chambersburg St. and remembered, "..the effect was enough to frighten us to death." Youngsters, like ten year olds Charles McCurdy and Gates Fahnestock, watched from the safety of their homes and thought it was, "..rather a leisurely and gentle entry and enjoyed it as if it were a wild west show."[34]

Upon reaching the square the horsemen wheeled about momentarily until orders barked by the officers sent squads charging out the intersecting streets. Once again they displayed a wild demeanor which badly frightened Tillie Pierce. When writing her memoirs she recalled her impressions of that scene: "What a horrible sight! There they were..clad almost in rags, covered with dust, riding wildly..down the street..shouting, cursing, brandishing their revolvers and firing right and left." This initial deployment did little more than capture a few horses being led out Baltimore Street near the Evergreen Cemetery, and precipitate a brief fire-fight with two of Bell's men who had not cleared the area. The latter resulted in the death of Pvt. George Sandoe, a local man, who had the tragic distinction of becoming the first soldier killed at Gettysburg.[35]

The strain was beginning to show on some of the citizens. The capture of the horses led to a flare up between two neighborhood families. Under normal circumstances it is unlikely that such an incident would have ever occurred. Among the boys caught by the Rebels leading away the animals was young Sam Wade, Jenny Wade's twelve year old brother. The Wade's were poor and Sam was living with the Pierce's as a "hired boy." As the procession of horses and their riders were being led back into town, it passed the Pierce house. Mrs. Pierce beckoned to one of the Confederates and called out:

"You don't want the boy! He is not our boy, he is only living with us."

The man replied, "No we don't want the boy, you can have him; we are only after the horses."

Nearby and watching this little drama was Jennie Wade, who lived a half block away on Breckenridge Street. According to Tillie, Jennie held the Pierce's responsible for little Sam's predicament and shouted a mild threat: "If the Rebs take our Sam, I don't know what I'll do with you folks!" Sam was released but the animal was not. A short time later, Mr. Pierce went to Col. White and pleaded for the return of the family's beloved horse. Colonel White refused. He had been informed, he said, that Pierce was, "..a black Abolitionist, and that he had two sons in the Union army, whom he supposed had taken as much from the south as they were taking from him." Tillie claimed that Jennie Wade had been the source of Col. White's information about her father's politics and family circumstances. She was clearly distressed by Jennie's, "..unkind disposition toward our family." She took her feelings a giant step forward and suggested that Jennie was a southern sympathizer.[36] This was the first of several occasions where a Gettysburg citizen would brand another as disloyal during the stress of those tumultuous days.

On the eastern end of town, the arrival of the Confederates stimulated more curiosity than fear in Sarah King. Her father was sitting by a window, engrossed in his newspaper, when the Rebels came galloping out York Street. Sarah yanked his attention back to the affairs in town with a loud shout, "Here they come!"

"Who," asked her startled father.

"The Rebs, don't you hear the yell."

The horsemen were passing the house in pursuit of Captain Bell, himself. Sarah and her children stood on the porch and watched the chase with wide eyed fascination. Her father's first thought was for the safety of the youngsters.

"Bring the children in and lock the door," he shouted to Sarah.

"No, I want them to see all they can of this," Sarah replied.

Sarah saw no danger and thought the whole event was history in the making. If not history it was certainly an exciting spectacle; with oaths, shouts and shots exchanged along the way. Soon the Confederates returned at a walk, having been out distanced by their quarry.[37] In a few more days, Sarah's children would be exposed to far more history than their mother could have ever imagined.

A half hour behind White's cavalry, General Gordon's Brigade of infantry marched into town along the Mummasburg Road. Their arrival signaled a new level of anxiety about the town's safety, despite assurances from the invaders that civilians and private property would not be molested. General Early was on the scene and he had sent advanced word that he intended to place a requisition for supplies upon the town. Everyone knew that most of the merchandise the Confederates would want had been shipped away to safety. The fear was the Rebels would revert to wholesale looting, or worse yet, burn the town in retaliation.[38]

General Early wrote out a list of foodstuff and supplies he required. Riding up Baltimore Street he met David Kendlehart, borough council president, in front of his home across from the courthouse. Early presented him with the requisition. Kendlehart, in turn, convened the town council in the law office of councilman William Duncan on the NW corner of the square. The meeting was inconclusive as to what they should do; with some advocating defiance and others urging compliance for fear of the consequences. Not getting a consensus on what to do from his fellow councilmen, Kendlehart took it upon himself to form a response. Accompanied by Alexander Buehler, he went in search of General Early whom he encountered near the 'Diamond', likely in front of Moses McClean's house on Baltimore Street. He told Early that it was impossible for the town to meet the demands, but that the Confederates were welcome to examine the merchants stores to see what they could find.[39] It was a timely stroke of diplomatic genius. Early was evidently satisfied with the compromise as there were no acts of retaliation.

Kendlehart was not all that confident about General Early's mood concerning his non-compliance to the demands. When a courier arrived at Kendlehart's front door later that evening with word that General Early wanted to see him, the suspicions overcame him. He had his daughter, Margaretta, tell the General's aide that he was not at home while he quietly slipped out the back door. He did not return home until after the Confederates had left the next day.[40]

The appearance of the Rebels confirmed their general need for clothes, hats and shoes. Michael Jacobs noted that they were dirty and ragged, hardly looking the part of "chivalrous southerners." Sarah King saw them more in the image of "Falstaff's recruits," which candidly captured her "sympathy." The parade of Early's men by her porch with their booty from the town's shelves made a lasting impression. In her reminiscences written years later, she vividly recalled the scene: "Some of the men had a pile of hats on their heads..strings of muslin and other goods trailing on the ground, the blankets, quilts and shawls were piled up on their horses.. altogether forming a laughable picture." Perhaps the epitome of need was illustrated when Albertus McCreary observed a trooper with spurs strapped onto his bare feet.[41]

It was no wonder that the soldiers eagerly descended upon the stores. They did not loot. Purchases were paid for with Confederate currency, although worthless to the hapless merchant supplying the goods. Young Charles McCurdy found himself unexpectedly benefitting from one such transaction.

Across from McCurdy's house on Chambersburg St. was "Petey" Winter's sweet shop. Like most other merchants, Winter had closed up before the Confederates arrived. His wares were not the type to go unnoticed and he was forced to reopen. This was too much drama for a ten year old to pass up. Fearless of the enemy soldiers, he went across the street to watch through the shop window. Shortly a trooper came out with his hat full of candy and, "..seeing a expectant looking small boy gazing enviously at his store, gave me a handful."[42]

Sweets were not the only commodity high on the soldiers want list. Whiskey had universal appeal in both armies. Sometime after dark a Lieutenant, accompanied by three privates, presented themselves at the Globe Inn demanding to purchase spirits. The officer "compelled" the proprietor, Charles Will, "..to roll out three barrels of whiskey." The enlisted men carried off the libation while the Lieutenant wrote out an order on the Confederate Government. Mr. Will refused to accept the paper.

"I want good money," he demanded.

"In two months our money will be better than yours as we may remain in your state an indefinite time," was the curt response.

Turning on his heel the Confederate officer departed to follow his men with their booty. The elder Will and his son John were left shaken with anger and the prospect that the Lieutenant's prediction might become a reality.[43]

There was a dark side to the Confederate occupation. The worst fears imaginable came true for many of the unfortunate black citizens who had not fled from town. Those who were caught were lined up on Chambersburg Street and marched away under guard, crying and moaning, presumably back to the south and slavery. At least one was able to escape from this awful procession. Aunt Liz, the David McCreary family's domestic, slipped away as the column of unfortunates began their march and hid for two days in the belfry of the Christ Lutheran Church.[44] White citizens helped others avoid capture. Mary Warren's mother took in a frantic black minister's widow and daughter and hid them above the kitchen in their West Middle Street home until the crisis passed.[45]

Aside from their seizure of the blacks, their unwanted "trade" with the merchants and their confiscation of horses, the Confederates committed no outrages on the town or its citizens. There were no confirmed instances of robbery or assault, although Sarah King reported a rumor that Adam Doersom, a local blacksmith, was accosted for money by a former apprentice, riding with the Confederates. In fact the regimental bands set up in the 'Diamond' in front of David Wills' house and serenaded the town with southern martial tunes including 'Dixie'. The concert was lively, but not particularly appreciated by the townspeople.[46]

War contraband was another matter. During the night seventeen railroad cars were moved a mile out of town and burned. The fire destroyed the rail bridge over Rock Creek. Of course the track was torn up and the telegraph wires severed.[47]

The next morning 36 prisoners from the 26th P.E.V. were brought out of the courthouse where they were kept overnight and paroled. Two officers were not released and were taken along with their captors. By 8:00 A.M. the Confederates were gone, headed east toward York.

The consensus opinion was that the Confederates had behaved rather gentlemanly. THE COMPILER in its June 29th publication declared: "Their deportment generally was civil." Fannie Buehler's account supports that conclusion. Overcoming her initial fear at being left alone in a town occupied by the enemy, she ventured out at dusk to sit on her front stoop. Two soldiers loitering in front of the courthouse wandered over to speak with her. They, "..asked permission to sit down," and engaged Fannie in a long conversation. They made quite a favorable impression. As Fannie recalled: " They were civil and well behaved..no bitterness was expressed by them or me." During the course of conversation they expressed surprise at the condition of things as they saw them in the north. They could not understand why there were so many young men not in the army. When Fannie explained that the northern manpower resource was almost limitless, they responded somewhat glumly, "Well we haven't as many men left in the south as you."[48] It is highly unlikely that anyone at the moment realized that their conversation had just touched on the central factor that would determine the ultimate outcome of the war.

The Rebels left the Jacobs family with a variety of impressions. Michael's recollections were pointed toward the impact they made on the senses. He recalled that when the Confederates arrived it had been raining and the air was heavy and, "..filled with the filthy exhalations from their bodies." His son Henry, was impressed by their behavior: "Those Confederates were very business-like in their attitude toward the townspeople, but were considerate enough."[49]

When the last Confederates departed on Saturday the 27th it brought forth a collective sigh of relief, but little abatement in excitement. Four scouts from Cole's Federal cavalry regiment rode into town from Emmitsburg, practically on the heels of the departing Rebels. Finding the Confederates gone, they suspended their scout and retired to the Globe Inn for refreshments. A short while later they were suddenly engaged in a dramatic chase after a stranger passing through town from the west. The wild ride, the exchange of shots and final capture were wartime drama played out along York Street before the townspeople's very eyes. The subdued intruder proved to be a Confederate chaplain carrying a message for General Early. A short time later another hapless messenger wandered into the same trap.[50] By mid afternoon the scouts left with their prisoners, and the town was left to itself to calm down and digest all the turmoil they had experienced over the past twenty four hours.

On Sunday the town rejoiced at the prospect of having a peaceful Sabbath, "..such as Gettysburg used to know."[51] Just as services ended a blue column of cavalry trooped over Baltimore Street hill and into the square, bringing with them a grim reminder of the close proximity of the warring armies. No matter, the security they brought was instantly embraced by the civilians. Agnes Barr recalled: "We were delighted to see them. All along the streets the people were out with their buckets of water and tin cups."[52] Catherine Foster's recollections of the event were more expansive: "Front doors and windows opened and brought out old and young and feeble alike to hail the Union troops with song and feed them with bread and pie. We now felt assured that our Government were keeping an eye on us."[53]

Not all citizens saw the day as reassuring as Catherine Foster. That evening Salome Myers recorded a contrasting view of the state of affairs in her diary: "(We) had no preaching. Rev. Isenberg has skedaddled. The town is pretty clear of darkies. They have nearly all left. I pity the poor creatures. Darkies of both sexes are skedaddling and some white folks of the male sex . . . Oh dear, I wish the excitement was over."[54]

To whatever extent it existed, the sense of security was short lived. First thing the next morning the troopers mounted up and left, going south towards Littlestown. When the last trooper passed out of sight over Cemetery Hill, Gettysburg was once again left alone to deal with it's fears and apprehensions. The collective mood of the town quickly turned somber.[55] A new source of anxiety was at work on their psyche. Since the Rebels came to town on Friday they were completely isolated from the outside world. The telegraph was out. No trains were arriving. No travelers, other than the cameo appearances of cavalry, were coming in on the roads. Enemy troops were thought to be all around. The foreboding campfires on the mountainside about Cashtown had reappeared.[56] The whereabouts of the Union army was unknown. THE COMPILER for June 29th addressed the situation with a dramatic understatement: "It is annoying to be thus isolated." A more accurate barometer of local emotions was undoubtedly captured by Catherine Foster when she wrote: "The suspense grew intolerable to which the battle itself proved a relief."[57]

One citizen decided to take action to relieve the apprehension. On the evening of the 29th, Samuel Herbst mounted a horse that somehow had escaped confiscation by Early's men, and headed down the Emmitsburg Road to try and find out some information on the whereabouts of the Union army. He returned later that night with "comforting assurances" that friendly forces were approaching. Alice Powers recalled: "The news flew through town like wildfire."[58]

If Tuesday, June 30th, dawned with a new sense of optimism for the town, it was quickly doused. Once more fate was playing a cruel game of teeter-totter with the collective emotions of Gettysburg.

By mid morning mounted Confederate officers appeared on the crest of Seminary Ridge. Sarah Broadhead saw them from her back porch. Infantry pickets moved closer toward the town, as near as Carrie Sheads' Oak Ridge Seminary on the Chambersburg Pike.[59] The dire news of the nearby presence of the Confederates spread rapidly.

Almost before that word could be passed to the east end of town, a column of blue clad horsemen came into view, moving northeast along the Emmitsburg Road. They were the vanguard of General John Buford's Ist Cavalry Division, Army of the Potomac. The hope and prayers generated by the news from Samuel Herbst's midnight ride had been fulfilled. Rejoicing replaced gloom in the hearts of the citizens as they got this new word.[60] The Confederate officers saw the Yankees at about the same time. Their pickets were recalled and the Rebels quickly disappeared from Seminary Ridge as they moved away from Gettysburg toward Cashtown from whence they had come.

When the head of the Union cavalry column reached the intersection with South Washington St. it turned left and proceeded north towards the town. Little did these tired and dusty troopers expect the glorious reception they were about to experience. [61] Unaware of what the past two weeks had been like for the townspeople, they had no way of knowing they were seen as knights in shining armor.

The citizens flocked to Washington Street. In almost no time, both sides were thronged with waving, shouting, men, women and children. The celebration continued for over an hour until the column had passed beyond the college campus and gone into camp. The entire time that the column was passing many of the young women of the town remained at the intersections at Breckenridge, W. High and W. Middle streets, welcoming the troopers with smiles and patriotic songs. [62]

Young boys ran along side of the big cavalry horses following them right into camp. There they remained for the rest of the day, admiring their new heros and helping out with menial chores such as watering the horses. [63] The whole event took on a circus atmosphere.

This spontaneous outpouring did not go unnoticed by the troopers. Capt. W.C. Hazelton, 8th Illinois, like many others in Buford's command, was overwhelmed by the reception. When recalling the scene 28 years later, he was still somewhat in awe: "Men, women and children crowded the side walks and vied with each other in demonstrations of joyous welcome. Hands were reached up eagerly to clasp the hands of our bronzed and dusty troopers. Cake, milk, water and beer were passed up to the moving column...Doors, windows and balconies were filled with ladies waving handkerchiefs. Altogether it was one of the most touching, spontaneous and heart-felt demonstrations my eyes ever witnessed...To receive such a reception under such circumstances as we did was an inspiration. It inspired us to heroic deeds."[64]

That evening many families invited troopers into their homes for supper. The guests, who were complete strangers to their grateful hosts, were treated like family. The Henry Garlach's fed numerous soldiers that day until the prepared food was exhausted. Henry told them all, "..to come back the next day and he would have a good dinner for them."[65]

The gala doings to the contrary, John Buford knew there was serious business at hand. He too had seen the Confederates to the west of town and suspected that Lee's entire army was in the immediate vicinity. In order to insure that the enthusiastic reception of the town did not unduly distract his men, he invoked some rules under martial law. Providing his troopers with any alcoholic beverages was strictly forbidden. THE SENTINEL presses were hired to print a bulletin so notifying the citizens and tavern owners. Even under the threat of "severe punishment," the prohibition was not totally successful. [66]

While Buford and his commanders might have been aware that big danger was imminent, the townspeople of Gettysburg were not. The signs seemed to be too obvious to have been ignored or misinterpreted, but by many they were. The evidence to that fact is recorded in a number of memoirs.

Perhaps it was a simple case of naivete. To the untrained eye the 3500 horsemen of Buford's command must have appeared to be as large as a entire army, just as Early's troops had a few days before. Catherine Foster believed this: "With the 6000(sic) cavalry between us and the enemy, we thought the battle was good as begun, fought and won." Charles McCurdy was aware of the complacency. He recalled: "..it does not seem that people realized the possibility of a battle at their doors. No restrictions were placed on my goings and comings. I was not warned to keep near home." Dan Skelly was another who commented on the town's almost whimsical attitude toward their situation. In his memoirs he noted: "..the people settled down (that night) in their homes with a sense of security ..and with little thought of what tomorrow had in store for them." Fifteen year old Tillie Pierce had almost the identical recollection of the prevailing mood in town that night: "As we lay down for the night little did we think what the morrow would bring forth." Albertus McCreary was emphatic: "Not..anyone even dreamed that a great battle would be fought near us..."[67]

Perhaps it was more than simple naivete. Perhaps it was a case of mental denial or numbness brought on by the constant strain of so many emotional highs and lows, particularly in the past three weeks. Fannie Buehler gives confirming insight into this theory in her reminiscences: "We were so used to the cry, "The Rebels are Coming," that we paid little attention to it..When they really came we were unprepared for them."[68]

JULY 1ST: "...an awful reality"

Dawn on July 1st arrived gloriously according to Catherine Ziegler's memory: "The sun shone in all it's splendor."[1] The townspeople arose and most began the day in their usual manner. Henry Jacobs recalled: "Gettysburg awoke and..was not alarmed." Professor Michael Jacobs was up early as usual and out in time to teach his 8 A.M. mathematics class at the college. Sarah Broadhead went about her plans to bake bread for the family. Charles Tyson walked the three blocks from his new house on lower Chambersburg St., to open his photographic gallery on York St.[2]

The young boys of the town such as Gates Fahnestock, Charles McCurdy, Leander Warren and others dispensed with the morning chores as quickly as possible and headed out to the cavalry camps to renew acquaintances with the troopers. Unexpectedly their adventure was prematurely interrupted by the sudden commencement of battle. Catherine Ziegler recalled the moment: "About 8 A.M. an ominous sound was heard that struck terror to the hearts of all..it was the call to battle."[3]

That bugle call marked the beginning of an event that would irreversibly change the course of destiny for Gettysburg and the lives of its citizens. When the shrill notes of the bugles faded a careful ear could pick up the distinct "pop, pop" of distant small arms fire. The sudden scramble by the troopers to fall-in was signal enough for Leander Warren and his companions to skedaddle for home.[4]

Back in Gettysburg there was a growing excitement along with a general sense of confusion and anxiety. People living in the northwest area of town, closest to the sounds of battle, began to come out of their houses into the streets. Anxiously they moved from group to group, asking one another what does this mean? Mary Horner, captured the mood in her reminiscences: "..few of us dreamed that our quiet village ..would be a battlefield." In fact the conception of a real battle was so foreign to many, that Mary overheard an acquaintance admonish some soldiers passing along the street: "Why do you come to town to have a fight? There are some old fields out there. Why don't you go out there?"[5]

At Sarah King's house at the corner of York and Liberty Streets, the situation was calmer. The initial sounds of battle had not reached the ears of those living on the opposite side of town from all the activity. Sitting on her front porch she watched as a single mounted trooper approached from the center of town. Seeing her when he came opposite the house, he shouted the warning:"Well, the ball is about to open." The warning was not lost on Sarah. She immediately jumped up and began packing, "..some things in case we had to leave." In just a few hours her foresight would serve her family well.[6]

On the south end of town the situation was similar to that on lower York Street. The first sounds of fighting went unnoticed. Families followed their normal morning rituals of breakfast and chores. Anna Garlach went early to the garden to pick green beans for a dinner the family expected to share with newly made friends in the Union cavalry regiments.[7] Their reprieve from the excitement and anxiety would be short lived. The Garlach's dinner party would be cancelled by the harshest of circumstances.

On the west end of town, nearest to the fighting, the scene was entirely different and the morale of the citizens there was rapidly deteriorating. The sounds of firing became more frequent and distinct. The fighting was moving closer. About 9 o'clock the artillery opened and fear replaced anxiety. From this moment the whole town was instantly aware that something terrible was unfolding in their midst.

Sarah Broadhead was just putting her bread in the oven when she heard the first boom of the cannon. Her first thoughts were reflective of her high level of anxiety; "..where to go, what to do?"[8] Salome Myers and several of her neighbors were overcome by fear and a sense of numbness: "Many of us sat on our doorsteps, our hearts beating with anxiety, looking at one another mutely."[9]

Strangely, fear seemed to foster an even stronger sense of curiosity. Many in town succumbed to the urge to watch the terrible drama that was threatening their very existence. A number of men and older boys started out to the ridges west of town to seek an unobstructed and close-up view of the action.

Chambersburg Pike looking west to Seminary Ridge

Daniel Skelly and a friend found the troopers preparing to move out from their camp beyond the college: "We were standing by Colonel Devin's tent when he received his orders (from Buford) to move his brigade west of town." The young men could not bring themselves to return to town. Instead they gave in to a strange, irresistible urge to follow the distant sound of firing. Cutting across fields they ended up on Oak Ridge near the unfinished railroad cut. A small group of men and boys were already there, watching the action unfold between McPherson's and Herr's ridges just to the west. In 1863 the area around the cut was all but bare of woods and individual trees stood out prominently. Daniel found a sturdy one and climbed up into the upper branches for a better view. He could see Confederate artillery on Herr's ridge, 3/4 of a mile away, firing rapidly on Union guns and dismounted troopers along the nearer McPherson's ridges. Suddenly horrible noises began to rend the air over the heads of the spectators. Errant Confederate shells were finding an unintended target. A stampede back to town began immediately. Skelly lingered, fascinated by the spectacle. Then a shell passed through the top branches of his perch. In his words: "I slipped down and joined the retreat."[10]

Young Charles McCurdy, who had gone out the Chambersburg Pike to visit the cavalrymen he had met the day before, was caught in a dangerous artillery impact zone. As he was wandering along the road, somewhat bewildered at the sudden change of events, a shell burst a few hundred yards away. Almost before he could react, his frantic father came running up and turned him toward the town. Together they ran all the way back to their Chambersburg Street home.[11]

William McClean, a young attorney with a family of two children, found himself drawn by the same fascination. Leaving his wife and children in their E. Middle Street home he headed out the Mummasburg Road. He rationalized to himself that he needed to check on the safety of his father's farm along the eastern base of Oak Ridge. The real lure was the top of the ridge which would offer a good view of the fields where the fighting was taking place. He, too, experienced the sudden shock of a shell exploding close by. His reaction was predictable: "..the shell had the effect of utterly removing all the curiosity I had entertained."[12] He quickly retraced his steps to his home and family.

From among the curious who ventured out onto the field that day, Catherine Ziegler found herself the closest to the action. The Zieglers occupied an apartment in the 1st floor of the Lutheran Theological Seminary building, where her father served as the caretaker. When the battle spread to the ridges just to the west, Catherine followed an impulse to watch the deadly pageantry. Years later, she recalled the scene: "I had always had a desire to see something of a battle..I quietly slipped from the house to the edge of the woods back (west) of the Seminary, and I was enjoying an awe inspiring scene, when a bullet flew so near my head that I could hear the whizzing sound it made. That sent me speeding home to the cellar."[13]

This phenomenon of grim curiosity prevailed in town as well. A number of men, women and children took to the roofs of their houses to try and gain a glimpse of the deadly conflict. They too were exposed to danger. Gettysburg was not a target of the Confederate gunners, but the town did lie behind the Union lines in the direct line of fire. Stray shells and spent bullets naturally found their way into the village. The close proximity of a passing missile was enough to bring about a quick retreat from the roof by Robert McClean and his younger sister Elizabeth. Robert never forgot the experience: "My curiosity, interest and gazing were all terminated by a passage overhead of a fierce sounding missile." His sister thought it sounded as if, "..the Confederates were firing pieces of railroad from their cannon." For young Gates Fahnestock, a similar experience just added to the excitement, and he was content to stay on his exposed perch until called down by the frantic pleas of his uncle Henry.[14]

A roof top observation perch served more than just the curiosity of the towns-people that morning. Sometime around 10:30, after he returned from his excursion to Seminary Ridge, Daniel Skelly found himself atop the Fahnestock Brothers' store building with several members of the Fahnestock family. There was an observation deck with benches and a railing at the rear of the flat roof. It provided a good view of the field where the battle was being fought. While they were there, Skelly noticed a Union General and his staff riding down Baltimore Street. The entourage stopped in front of the courthouse. Several of the staff officers attempted to reach the belfry. They were unsuccessful. Skelly hurried down to the street and told them they could see the battle action from the Fahnestock roof. They were welcome to use the facility. The invitation was accepted at once. The General was Oliver O. Howard, commander of the Union 11th Corps, who had just arrived from Em-mitsburg in advance of his troops. The grateful General calmly surveyed the fields west and north of the town, ignoring the presence of the deadly missiles in the air. Soon a courier galloped up W. Middle Street and reined in below the party on the roof. He shouted up to Howard the news that General Reynolds had been killed and that the General's immediate presence on the field was required. In an instant Howard and his staff were gone, leaving behind a slightly bewildered Daniel Skelly to ponder the dramatic events unfolding in the town's midst.[15]

Catherine Foster, whose house sat on the N.W. corner of High and S. Washing-ton Streets, watched the distant drama from her second story, rear balcony. Earlier, General John Reynold's and his staff had passed by on Washington Street, and paused to warn Catherine and her cousin, Belle Stewart, of the danger. He urged them to go into the cellar. The General's humane concern was appreciated, but his advice was ignored. Fascinated by the sights, the women remained in this exposed position for several hours, discounting the danger from the "hissing shells." During that time Catherine found at least one scene that provided a momentary break in an otherwise frightful pageant. Immediately following the opening of the artillery fire, she witnessed the amusing spectacle of the Seminary students fleeing wildly towards the town, "..at a speed greater than the double quick." Despite this comic respite the situation was deadly serious. Shortly before noon she and Belle were drawn down to the street as the 11th Corps troops began passing by. No sooner had Catherine walked out her front door when a shell crashed into the rear balcony, "..completely destroying it."(16) Timing is everything. Catherine Foster avoided, by mere minutes, the dubious distinction of depriving fellow townsperson, Jennie Wade, of her lasting fame as the only civilian killed at Gettysburg..

By mid morning the town was beginning to lose its grip on maintaining any sense of normalcy. At the College, Professor Jacobs gave up trying to compete with the growing excitement for the attention of his students, and dismissed his class with the declaration: "We will close and see what is going on for you know nothing about the lesson anyhow." Charles Tyson emerged from his darkroom, where he was processing a picture taken earlier that morning, to discover his shop had emptied of waiting customers. This was about 10 o'clock.(17)

There were a few instances where the attitude of business-as-usual still prevailed. At the Fahnestock Brothers store, Mary Felty was taking delivery on a fine set of English china while errant shells passed overhead.(18) The Globe Inn was doing a brisk business in whiskey sales to cavalrymen. This trade was halted shortly thereafter by intervening officers, not by a shortage of demand.(19)

The intensity of the fighting grew with each passing hour. By 10 o'clock the first wounded began to trickle into the west end of town. The initial reaction of the townspeople was one of shock and horror. The effect on Salome Myers typified the personal experience recalled in many existing memoirs: "..three men came up the street. The middle one could barely walk. His head had been hastily bandaged and blood was visible. I grew faint with horror."(20)

Down on Chambersburg Street the reaction at the John Scott house was much the same. Mary McAllister recalled the scene: "The first wounded soldier I saw was with John McClellan..The soldier was on a white horse and John was holding him by the leg. The blood was running down out of the wound over the horse. Our John (Scott) had been sick and was just able to be about and he fainted (at the sight)." McClellan brought the horse and wounded man to the curb in front of the house next door (Belle King's) and called out, "Belle, come out here and help this man." McClellan, with the help of Belle King and Mary McAllister got the man down and let the horse go. They brought him into the Scott's house and "put him on the lounge." Mary was in a state of shock: "I did not know what to do!"(21)

Out of the shock emerged a new energy and purpose. Many of the women of the

The Christ Lutheran Church ca 1910 (GNMP)

town turned to the humanitarian needs of the hour. The arriving wounded were taken into homes and given caring, if not professional, ministration. Neighbors, Mary McAllister and Nancy Weikert, along with her 19 year old niece Amanda Reinecker, hurried across Chambersburg Street to the Christ Lutheran Church and opened its doors to accommodate the arriving wounded. They remained and assisted the surgeons until exhaustion and concern for personal safety forced them to return home during the Union retreat through town.[22]

This was a scene that was repeated all over town as the need for space to treat the wounded opened more churches and public facilities. The miracle in all of this was the ability of these volunteer women to immediately overcome their natural repulsion to the mutilation and suffering of the wounded and perform such gruesome, but life sustaining work.

There was at least one exception that requires no apology. Twelve year old Mary Montfort accompanied her mother, Sarah, to a warehouse near the railroad to help with the wounded. Soon after arriving, Mary came across her own soldier/father lying conscious with a gaping hole in his side made by a shell fragment. He had fallen in battle, practically within sight of his home and family. Mary recorded the scene in her diary: "Father looked at me and said, "Mary Elizabeth," then he closed his eyes...Mother told me to go home and take care of Grandma and Jennie Ann (her little sister)." With nothing more than a final kiss bestowed upon her father's brow, Mary left and made her way home, trying to comprehend the pain and grief this battle had so suddenly bestowed upon her.[23]

Those women not involved directly in caring for the wounded turned to picking lint and preparing bandages. This activity was undertaken in groups gathered in private homes. It proved to be a vital resource for the doctors and served to take the women's minds off their own exposure to danger.

About 10:30 the Union infantry entered the fight around McPherson's farm and the noise of battle and volume of missiles falling in the town escalated. Union officers rode up Chambersburg Street warning of the dangers of Confederate artillery, urging the residents to leave for a safer part of town. Sarah Broadhead, the Gilberts, the Tysons, all living on the lower end of the street, followed the advice. Some living closer to the center of town followed suit.

Charles Tyson and his bride of two months exemplified the tug between a pragmatic need to seek immediate safety and the emotional ties to certain personal property. His wife Maria, anticipating the need to abandon their house on lower Chambersburg Street, had packed a trunk of valuables, including their wedding clothes. While the shells screeched overhead, her husband dragged out the trunk and worked it into a wheelbarrow. Pushing the trunk before him, Charles and Maria started up the street towards the 'Diamond'. They had struggled, "..only a short distance," before his next door neighbor, William Boyer, came by with a horse and wagon. Together they hoisted the Tyson's trunk on the back. Charles, "..tumbled the wheelbarrow over into Mr. Chritzman's yard" and away they went at an accelerated pace.

They went first to a location on lower Baltimore Street which at that time was out of the way of the immediate danger. Later in the day, when people were being advised (falsely as it turned out) that the Confederates might shell the town, the Boyers and Tysons left via the Hanover Road. They eventually worked their way to Littlestown, ten miles south of Gettysburg.[24]

Charles McCurdy's family hastily packed a few belongings and headed for his aged grandmother's house (Ann McCurdy's) on the top of Baltimore Street hill. It was a trip of less than four blocks, but they perceived themselves to be safer there.[25]

Mary Horner gathered her two children and left their house seeking safety. First she went out to the College campus north of town to stay with President Henry Baugher's family. This area soon turned into a battle zone. Mary and her hosts returned to town seeking a more secure location. Finally during the retreat of the Union forces through town, she accepted an invitation from Mary Carson, the wife of Duncan Carson, Teller for the Gettysburg Bank, to sit out the danger in the safety of the bank's vault. Even there the horrors of the combat reached them. Mrs Carson's brother, an officer in the 5th Maine Battery, fell with a bullet in his leg while defending Seminary Ridge. He was carried from the field and, by his own direction, taken to his sister's house adjacent to the bank. He ended up in the vault along with the others. Mary, her children and seventeen other refugees in the vault, had to witness close up the horror and pain of battle.[26]

Others took the warnings to seek safety as the omen to flee town. Taking only the barest of essentials a number of families hastily left by roads to the east and south. Included were Sarah King and her family, the Charles Tysons, the William Boyers, the Catherine Ziegler family and Tillie Pierce (her family stayed) along with her next door neighbor, Mrs George Schriver and her two daughters. The exodus included nearly all the black residents who did not leave, or left and came back, at the time of the earlier Confederate visit on June 26th.

To stay or to leave their homes was naturally an agonizing decision for the civilians to make. The Jacob Hollinger family, whose brick house sat in the fork formed by the junction of the York and Hanover Roads, faced the dilemma. It was early afternoon and the fighting was spreading to the northeast of the town. Liberty Hollinger had just returned from her father's warehouse at Stratton Street and the railroad. Her aunt Sally Diehl was there on her way out of town. The Hollinger's were not inclined to leave and aunt Sally was urging Liberty's mother to go with her. Liberty recalled that her aunt was, "..amazed that we were not going to leave such an exposed place." Mrs Diehl was apparently successful in persuading the family to reconsider their position before she departed. While the Hollingers were standing around and deliberating what to do, two wounded Union officers walked up to the house. Liberty asked them for their professional advice. The officers recommended that they take to their cellar and ride out the fighting at home. The advice was accepted and the officers moved on towards Cemetery Hill. It would prove to be a wise decision for the Hollingers, as they were able to protect much of their property over the next several days.[27]

Since safety was the immediate concern for those who chose to leave, little thought was given as to the fate of their houses and belongings. Fate was cruel. The Confederates widely ransacked abandoned homes during their occupation of the town. Many lost all that they had. In the overall, "..the greater number of families stayed," substantially limiting the amount of Confederate looting.[28]

Not all citizens leaving Gettysburg that day were acting to flee the danger of battle. Mid morning, 68 year old John Burns stepped out of his house at the western end of Chambersburg Street armed with an old musket. Burns was determined to go out to the field and join the Union ranks. Upon seeing Joseph Broadhead up the street he admonished his neighbor to get a gun and to come along and fight for his country. When Broadhead refused Burns lit into him, challenging his courage, berating him with names such as "coward" and "chicken-hearted." Mary Slentz,

Burns' immediate neighbor to the east, heard the tirade and came out of her house to scold him for his behavior and advise him to stay out of the fight and remain at home. Burns would have none of it and went on his way toward the Seminary and the battlefront. He had more important adversaries to contest, and for his patriotic zeal he would suffer three wounds that afternoon.

All of this encounter was witnessed by twelve year-old Will Tipton and a group of his friends who were at the intersection of the Pike and Chambersburg Street hoping for a glimpse of the pageantry of war at a safe distance. Burns' antics surely added to their excitement, but soon fear, generated from the sound of missiles passing overhead and din of battle, sent them on a hasty retreat back up the street to their homes.[29]

While some residents were leaving, the Union 11th Corps was arriving. For those living along S. Washington Street the scene was deja vu with Buford's entry into town the day before. The appearance of so many troops rekindled feelings of security.[30]

Again the residents turned out to greet and cheer their saviors. Albertus McCreary and some companions ran down to the corner of High and S. Washington Streets and perched on the plank fence enclosing Eyster's Young Ladies Seminary to watch the pageant and cheer the troops. To these boys, the several thousand soldiers filling the street from pavement to pavement, looked like a whole army. Young McCreary turned to his companions and declared: "..there are enough soldiers here to whip all the Rebs in the south."[31]

This youthful miscalculation would soon become apparent to Albertus and all the rest of the town.

On both sides of the street people were handing out tin cups of water to parched and nearly exhausted soldiers, who were moving up Washington Street at the double time. Catherine Foster recalled: "..frequently officers asked us to stop providing water since there was no time to drink." Foster, and others such as the Powers sisters just across the street, paid the officers no heed. Meanwhile the soldiers were returning the kindness of the citizens with reassuring promises. Catherine Foster recalled one such sentiment expressed by a grateful recipient of a cool tin of water: "We are coming home to fight the Rebels from your door, and we'll drive them or we'll die."[32]

By 1 P.M. the 11th Corps had passed through town and deployed across the broad fields just to the north of the College. As they advanced toward Oak Ridge between the Mummasburg Road and the Harrisburg Pike the fighting spread and took on a new fury. The wounded began to come in from the front in such numbers that Leander Warren at first supposed, "..the whole army was falling back."[33] The rising number of wounded required more shelter facilities and more volunteers to provide pre and post operative care. To both these needs the town and its citizens responded. In addition to the churches and public buildings, including the school house on E. High Street, the proprietors of the large warehouse facilities opened their doors to the wounded. More and more private houses became makeshift hospitals. Many more of the town's women, like Mary McAllister and others before them, overcame their personal fears and natural repulsion to gore and human misery, and stepped forward to serve as nurses. Others chipped in and carried water into the newly created hospitals. Daniel Skelly recalled his own experiences: "Miss Julia Culp and I went to the courthouse with buckets of water. Quite a number of townspeople were there doing everything they could ..as the wounded were carried in."[34]

In the midst of all the frantic activity of civilian and military personnel moving to and fro through the town, a regimental band deployed in the 'Diamond' and played a repertoire of patriotic tunes. Robert McClean, living just a half block away on Baltimore Street, reacted to this "incongruity" with mixed emotions: "I remember how grating on the ear were the sounds of music..as the crimson stained warriors poured into the town from the front. Among the songs played was 'Dixie.' The intent, no doubt, was to cheer up the wounded." Elizabeth McClean also remembered the band playing in the square when recalling her experiences some 45 years later. To Elizabeth: "The 'Star Spangled Banner' sounded like a funeral dirge and brought tears to my eyes." Her depressed state of mind may have been influenced by the shock she had experienced earlier while watching a soldier at the horse trough in front of her house, grimly washing a hand shot through by a musket ball.[35]

There was one incident when civilian morale was given a momentary boost. Shortly after noon, a column of sullen, dejected and ragged Confederates were marched under guard down West Middle Street and then out Baltimore Street towards Westminster. Henry Jacobs rejoiced in the moment: "The streets held excitement enough for anyone and thrills of patriotic happiness..when we saw Archer's Brigade brought in."[36]

The spread of fighting brought more than just an increase of wounded into Gettysburg to traumatize the citizens. The volume of shells and bullets falling into town grew dramatically. In mid afternoon, just after the retreat by Union forces had begun, a shell plowed into the roof of the Christ Lutheran Church on Chambersburg Street. Inside the wounded and volunteer nurses were momentarily overcome with fear. Someone shouted out: "They are going to shell the church." That was enough for Mary McAllister, already exhausted from several hours of providing heart rending care for torn and dying boys. Despite the pleas from the army doctors to stay, she gathered herself and went out the front door to go to her house directly opposite the church. Hands from soldiers gathered outside the door tried to restrain her, fearing she would be harmed by the mob of retreating soldiers in the street below. Mary squirmed to free herself, crying out, "Oh, I want to go home!" The hands let go. With great difficulty she worked her way through the mass of soldiers moving along the street. The crush of soldiers flowing towards the square, some carrying wounded on their backs, pushed her a half a block beyond her house before she gained the other side in front of Buehler's drugstore. Upon reaching her house she had to cross over a front step, "..covered with blood." Gripped by a numbing sense of foreboding, she stepped inside, "..expecting to find all dead."[37]

She found instead a house full of soldiers, wounded and unwounded. Pushing through the crammed dining room she came into a kitchen full of exhausted men,

The Scott/McAllister house (center) on Chambersburg St. ca 1885 (ACHS)

most unhurt and seeking refuge from the deadly storm of enemy missiles. A Lt. Dailey was there with a sword taken earlier that morning from the captured Confederate General James Archer. With his own capture imminent, Dailey asked Mary to hide his trophy from the enemy. She complied. Also in the crowded kitchen was a slightly wounded Col. Henry A. Morrow, commander of the 24th Michigan. He passed his diary to Mary saying, "Here, I don't want them to get it." For want of a better place she loosened her bodice and put it in her dress. Martha Scott brought the colonel a civilian coat in hopes that the disguise would help him avoid capture. To Martha's dismay, Morrow shook his head, "He would not disguise himself." A short time later the Confederates entered the house and removed the unharmed and the ambulatory wounded. They did not recover Archer's sword or Col. Morrow's diary. The seriously injured were left behind, turning the Scott house into a hospital for days to come. In order to signify themselves as a humanitarian station, they hung one of Martha's red shawls out the upstairs window. Soon, many houses were showing a red flag.[38]

Between 3:30 and 4:00 P.M. the first elements of the retreating 11th Corps began to come in along the streets from north of town. The initial trickle of men quickly grew to a flood of frantic humanity accompanied by gunshots, hand to hand fighting and violent death in the streets, alleys and yards. With them came a new level of danger, confusion and fear for civilians. Mary Horner recalled: "During all the hours of this first day the horrors of war were being more and more familiar to us."[39] The hour between 4 to 5 o'clock provided the graduate course in the learning process.

The initial signs of a retreat were the return of the artillery caissons and wagons at the gallop. Salome Myers and her companions were at first puzzled as to what this meant. Then Federal officers began to ride through the streets ordering: "Women and children to the cellars. The Rebels will shell the town." The Myers family quickly complied and invited a number of their neighbors to join them in their spacious cellar.[40]

A short distance away, Catherine Foster stood in her front doorway and witnessed the growing tide of men, horses and wagons surge, "pell mell," up Washington Street. She observed men dropping out of the pack, "..into every nook and corner," to avoid the danger of bullets flying after them. She called out to one soldier passing by to inquire as to, "what this meant?"

"Don't be alarmed, we are only changing front," was the hasty reply.

The answer was hardly reassuring as pursuing Confederates could be seen a little more than a block away and bullets grazed her skirts. That was enough. Catherine quickly locked her front door and headed to the cellar to join the rest of the family. As she reached the head of the stairs a Union soldier (Cpl. Leander Wilcox, 151st PA) came in the rear door. There was no time for social exchanges. After locking the rear door, Catherine herded him down the steps. Cpl. Wilcox would remain hidden in the Foster's basement until liberated on July 4th.[41]

Over on Baltimore Street the scene was the same. From his grandmother's house Charles McCurdy witnessed: "..a wild and unorganized mob of blue clad soldiers, most of whom had thrown away their guns," running up the street.[42] Just a half block to the north, the David McCreary household was sitting down to a early supper when all the noise and confusion summoned them to their porch on the High Street side of the house. They witnessed the same scene of Union soldiers running and pushing each other, sweaty and black from powder and dirt. Some called for water and the McCreary's busied themselves to comply. In their haste to help, they lost sight of their own immediate danger. A sudden command brought an instant reminder. An officer rode up to the porch and shouted, "..all you good people go down into your cellar or you will be killed." Looking up, Albertus observed blue and gray clad soldiers engaged, "..in hand to hand conflicts," not a half block away. The McCrearys quickly obeyed.[43]

The blue wave of retreating soldiers and vehicles passed on over Baltimore Street hill towards the haven of fortifications and reserve support on Cemetery Hill. Half way down the south side of Baltimore Street hill, along the west pavement, sat the two story brick house and cabinetmaker's shop of the Henry Garlach family. Eighteen year old Anna Garlach watched the procession roll by from the upstairs, bedroom window. It made an impression she would never forget: "..there were more people in the street than I have ever seen since at any time. The street seemed blocked. In front of our house the crowd was so great that I believe I could have walked across the street on the heads of the soldiers." Some of the men saw her and implored her to seek shelter: "Go to the cellar, go to the cellar." Moved to action Anna, her mother Catherine, and her two brothers Will and baby Frank, quickly sought shelter in the cellar of their next door neighbor, Henrietta Schriver. Their own held a foot of water. Henry Garlach had left earlier in the day for the crest of Cemetery Hill to better observe the fighting. He suddenly found himself cut off from returning home by the retreat and the pursuit of the Rebels. His wife and children would go it alone for the duration of the battle.[44]

While units of the 11th Corps were in town trying to get south to Cemetery Hill, the 1st Corps line along Seminary Ridge collapsed. A hasty withdraw toward Cemetery Hill from the west began immediately. The line of retreat brought many of the troops, cannon, and wagons from the right wing of the 1st Corps into the western edge of town, adding to the confusion and congestion already crowding the streets. The Confederates followed close behind, bringing more fighting into the streets, alleys, and yards.

The impact on the civilians was predictable. Sarah Broadhead's experience and reaction was typical of most when suddenly confronted with the defeat of their army and the advance of the enemy into town: "I, with others, was sitting on the doorstep bathing wounds..all was bustle and confusion. No one can imagine in what extreme fright we were in when our men began to retreat." Just then a citizen galloped up and shouted to Sarah: "For God's sake go in the house. The Rebels are in the other end of town and all will be killed." She immediately heeded the warning. History has provided no clue as to the identity of Gettysburg's Paul Revere.[45]

When the Confederates entered the town the situation turned vicious. The citizens suddenly disappeared into the cellars, often accompanied by soldiers cut off in the retreat. Outside many of the Union soldiers were blocked by the congestion in the main streets and were captured or they turned into alleys and yards to fight off their relentless pursuers. For the few citizens who caught glimpses of this deadly pageant from their cellar windows, the sight brought new heights of horror. For those who could not see, but could hear the shouts and shots, the suspense and fear was agonizing.

What they saw was beyond their imagination; fighting and killing in their town's streets. In the basement of the Jacobs family, Henry looked out onto Washington Street and witnessed what to him must have been the cruelest form of murder. As he later recalled it, an exhausted Union soldier was dragging along at the best pace he could muster. Although still carrying his rifle he was making no signs of turning on his pursuers. The Confederates chasing him were just a few steps behind. Capture seemed easy enough. Instead a command, "..shoot him, shoot him," was given. The command was executed and the Union soldier pitched forward on the street and lay still, shot dead through the back.[46]

Nearby, Catherine Foster peeked out her cellar window and saw only men in gray cloth uniforms, "..their leader hatless, yelling furiously and firing, curdling one's blood."[47]

Just a half block away Salome Myers and family huddled in the darkness of their cellar and listened. They all, "..knelt shivering and prayed. The noise above our heads, the rattling of muskets, the unearthly cries mingled with the sobbing of the children, shook our hearts." Several houses to the west, Alice Powers witnessed the bloody, violent fight that was the source of the trauma suffered by the Myers family in their cellar. The 150th PA. was brought to bay in the middle of High Street and fought furiously to defend their colors. In just a few minutes they were overwhelmed, leaving several dead on the street and many more prisoners.[48]

At the east end of the block, the McCreary family had barely settled into their cellar when they heard the sound of fighting all around their house. Through the small cellar windows the light cast shadows on the opposite walls of men rushing back and forth. Albertus recalled: "Those shadows filled us with horror." Coupled with the shadows was the continuous noise of rifle shots and shouts. Holding back his fear, Albertus climbed up to one of the windows and looked out onto Baltimore Street. At just that moment a cannon unlimbered and fired down the street (toward the square) trying to hold back the pursuers: "What a noise it made and how the dust did fly." Soon they heard the sound of running feet on the porch they had just vacated. A voice called out in a loud command: "Shoot that fellow going over the fence." A shot banged loudly right by a window. In silent horror they imagined the fate of the poor boy seeking to escape over their backyard fence.[49]

One block nearer to the square, on E. Middle Street, the William McClean family for some unknown reason did not make it into their basement. Instead they huddled together in the dark, "..on a little, narrow platform at the head of the cellar stairs, behind the door, as we did not know what would happen next. Imagine what emotions were wrought in the little flock." William had left a pail of water on the front pavement for the retreating soldiers. When the Confederates arrived they loudly cautioned each other that it had been poisoned. The McCleans feared they would be summarily killed for this mistaken assumption.[50]

A block to the west of McClean's house, remnants of the 19th Indiana infantry turned into W. Middle Street from S. Washington, heading for Baltimore Street. A lieutenant was limping along with the group trying to keep pace. About mid block he fell hopelessly behind and turned into the areaway between the Skelly and Bowen houses. He found a open cellar door at the side of the Bowen house. Methodically he took off his sword and pistol belt and painfully climbed down to hide his arms. He emerged just as some Confederates ran into the yard from the street and surrounded him. They demanded his surrender, but were willing to kill. Emotions were running high on both sides and in that moment life hung by a thread. Daniel Skelly proudly recalled what happened next: "My mother intervened, offering to dress his wound first. The Confederates agreed and never came back for him. We hid him from capture the whole time."[51]

There was another near explosive confrontation, where the instant action and incredible bravery of a civilian woman served to defuse the situation and bring about a nonviolent resolution. At Carrie Sheads' Oak Hill Seminary, a group of men from the 97th N.Y. Infantry had been brought to bay and surrounded by pursuing Confederates. Recognizing that further resistance would result in unnecessary casualties, Col. Charles Wheelock signaled their surrender. In the ensuing confusion many of the vanquished, including Col. Wheelock, crowded into the Sheads' cellar, out of harms way from the many bullets still flying about, as the remainder of the 1st Corps continued their retreat toward the town. Armed Confederates entered the cellar to formalize the surrender and remove the captives. A Rebel sergeant, commanding the detail, confronted Col. Wheelock and demanded he surrender his sword, the universal gesture of capitulation. While he had ordered the surrender of his men, the Colonel apparently could not bear the implied humiliation of submitting to a noncommissioned officer. Wheelock responded by attempting to break the blade over his knee in open defiance of his captor's order. He failed and his action served to infuriate the sergeant. The Rebel drew his revolver and repeated his command, adding a threat to shoot the Colonel if he did not comply immediately. At this point Carrie Sheads entered the cellar and observed the standoff of wills that was about to result in a violent death. Ignoring the potential danger of intervening at such a moment, she hurried over to the two men and began pleading with them to resolve the issue in a way that would spare further bloodshed. Her effort was successful. The critical moment passed without violence. At that instant the sergeant's attention was called to another part of the cellar. Carrie used this opportunity to take the object of dispute from Wheelock, hide it in the folds of her skirts, and step away. The sergeant returned after only a short time and renewed his demand for the sword. Wheelock explained that he had given it to another Confederate in the sergeant's absence. This explanation was accepted and the Colonel and his men were marched away to a holding area. Carrie turned to tending the many wounded which would turn her school building into a makeshift hospital for the foreseeable future.[52]

Out on the eastern edge of town, the Hollinger family sat in the cellar of their brick home, safe from the bullets they could hear thudding into their upstairs walls. Perhaps Liberty Hollinger's recollections of that hour best described the situation, and expressed the state of mind for all citizens of Gettysburg: "We watched through the cellar windows and Oh, what horror filled our breasts as we gazed upon their bayonets and heard the deafening roar of musketry. Yes, we were really in the midst of an awful reality."[53]

Like a summer thunderstorm, the violent clashes subsided almost as suddenly as they began. The crest of the retreat washed over the town and then ebbed on the northern slopes of Cemetery Hill. A strange and momentary silence prevailed. Anxious families, almost afraid to move, stayed in their cellars and wondered what would happen next.

The McCreary family were jolted out of their trance by the sudden intrusion of light from the opening of the outer cellar door. While still adjusting their eyes to the bright light, five Confederate soldiers jumped down into their midst. The shock was paralyzing. The collective thought was, "..our last day had come." Some of the women began to cry and all, "..stood rooted to the spot in fear." David McCreary stepped forward and asked their intentions. The Confederates replied that they were looking for Yankees. Stating the obvious, McCreary assured them that, "..there were none here." The Confederates insisted on searching the entire house and to the astonishment of the family, thirteen Union soldiers were found hiding. The discovery created an awkward situation and anxiety began to rise. David McCreary turned to a time honored custom for entertaining visitors, practiced on both sides of the Mason-Dixon Line, to defuse the situation. He invited all parties to sit down and eat. The family supper, fully prepared and untouched, was still on the table. A reasonably social repast was enjoyed by everyone. Albertus used the interlude to collect names and addresses of the captured and promised to notify their kin. When the meal was over the Confederates left with their prisoners.[54]

Albertus McCreary house, ca 1870. (ACHS)

As incongruous as it may seem, that mortal enemies could suddenly stop killing one another and almost instantly return to civil fraternization, the scene at the McCreary house was not an isolated event. It happened in the Martin Stoever and Fannie Buehler houses. It undoubtedly happened elsewhere, but went unrecorded. (55)

Even before the last Union soldier gained the protective heights of Cemetery Hill, the Confederates began the search for those many who had been cutoff and were now fugitives hiding in every place imaginable. They were to be found in almost every building in town. The healthy were taken out and placed in a holding area near the College. The severely wounded were temporarily left where they were found, until care could return them to the ranks of the ambulatory.

The latter situation occurred at the Henry Stahle home. Stahle, who was the editor and publisher of the democratic weekly, THE COMPILER, was hosting a badly wounded Col. William W. Dudley of the 19th Indiana Infantry. Also with Stahle were Elizabeth and Jacob Gilbert, neighbors of Sarah Broadhead, who had fled lower Chambersburg Street for safer quarters at the beginning of the fighting. Mrs. Gilbert was ministering Col. Dudley who was in considerable pain from his leg wound. Confederates came to the house and searched it. Finding Dudley unable to move, they left him in the care of Stahle and the Gilberts. As time passed the pain became unbearable and Dudley implored Stahle to bring a surgeon. Stahle left and went across the street into the courthouse to seek a doctor. He finally succeeded in getting a Confederate surgeon, accompanied by a guard, to return to his house. The wound was treated and Dudley's condition was stabilized. This act of humanity probably saved the Colonel's life and, as events unfolded during the days immediately following the battle, it nearly cost Stahle his freedom.[56]

At Fannie Buehler's house a loud ringing of the front door bell interrupted the meal she was serving to the Union soldiers who had sought refuge in her house. Opening the door she was confronted by a group of Confederates led by Col. Harry Gilmor, temporarily acting as the Provost Marshal in Gettysburg. They announced that they were there to search for "concealed" Union soldiers. Fannie was a proud woman and took offense to the inference of being deceitful by hiding fugitives. She responded with a defiant retort: "There are Union soldiers in my house, but none of them are concealed." She stood aside and the Confederates entered. Right away there was a moment of surprise for the soldiers of both sides. Several recognized each other from an earlier time along the Rappahannock River in Virginia, where they had fraternized while on picket duty. For awhile the strange scene took on the air of a reunion. Then it was back to business. Fannie led the Rebels on a complete tour of her house while they searched every nook and cranny; even to the cellar, thereby exposing her ample larder of foodstuff to discovery. Miraculously the Confederates ignored the food and left with only the hardy captives in tow. The wounded were allowed to remain in Fannie's care, with the promise that they (the Rebels) would return for them later, ". . but they never returned, and we never saw them again."[57] Fannie then began the task of nursing and feeding her wards that would not end for two weeks.

Charles McCurdy's mother, Mary, did resort to a subtle deceit in an attempt to spare two soldiers who she knew were hiding in her mother-in-law's cellar. She and Charles had come out into the front yard of the elder Mrs. McCurdy's house, (on Baltimore St.) when the Confederate search party arrived. The Rebel's addressed Mary as to whether any soldiers were hiding inside "her house." She responded to the effect that she was not aware that any Union soldiers were hiding in "her house" (the McCurdy family lived on Chambersburg St.). It was a technically truthful answer, intended to mislead. Unfortunately, it did not work.[58]

Not all the Union soldiers who sought refuge in citizen's houses were discovered and captured. Those that avoided detection during the initial and subsequent Confederate sweeps were sustained by their protectors at great personal risk. It is impossible to determine exactly how many escaped capture by successfully hiding out in Gettysburg. It is this researcher's guess that the number was close to several dozen.

The most famous of these battle fugitives was Brig. Gen. Alexander Schimmelfennig, temporary commander of the 3rd Division, 11th Corps which fought on the fields north of Gettysburg. Trying to make his way through the town to Cemetery Hill, Gen. Schimmelfennig found himself trapped in a dead end alley at the rear of the Henry Garlach house. Pursuing Confederates entered the head of the alley and shot his horse from under him. Jumping up unharmed, the General climbed over the board fence by the barn and headed across the back yard toward the front of the house and Baltimore Street. Upon passing along- side of the house it became apparent that the Confederates controlled the street. His pursuers were beginning to climb the fence to his rear, so the diminutive General crawled under a covered drainage ditch in the yard to the side of the house in a final effort to avoid capture. There he escaped detection until nightfall arrived. Sometime after dark, Schimmelfennig backed his way out from the ditch cover and sought a less confining shelter. He settled on a spot along the front of a woodshed, standing just to the rear of the Garlach's kitchen. Here he squeezed himself between a double stack of firewood and a hog swill barrel. A short time later, when Catherine Garlach stopped to dip her slop bucket in preparation to feeding the family hogs, the General revealed his

The Garlach woodshed where Gen. Schimmelfennig hid, ca 1905. (ACHS)

presence to her. Upon overcoming her initial alarm, Catherine agreed to supply him with food and water on her next feeding trip. She made good on her promise the next day despite the fact that her yard was within the Confederate's advanced skirmish line. With this help, General Schimmelfennig remained undetected in his hide out until early in the morning of July 4th, when he emerged to rejoin his comrades following the Confederate withdrawal.[59]

There were other situations where citizens acted spontaneously and bravely to help a soldier-fugitive avoid capture and imprisonment. Catherine Foster and her cousin Belle Stewart combined quick think-

Catherine Garlach, ca 1885. (GRB)

ing with brazen audacity to save Cpl. Wilcox from certain capture. They were in the act of concealing the Corporal when the outer cellar door was yanked open and two Confederate soldiers, accompanied by an officer, came down. The atmosphere turned thick with tension.

"Are there any Yankees here?"

The two women deftly placed themselves between the intruders and Wilcox's hiding place under a potato bin, while Catherine anxiously replied: "We are all here, suppose you call us all Yankees."

The diversion worked. The officer relaxed and kindly explained that he meant, "Yankee soldiers." Glancing about him, it was readily apparent that all those in the cellar were civilians. He then directed his men, who were probing close to Wilcox's thinly covered lair, to search the upstairs. The party moved to the upper floors leaving Cpl. Wilcox safely behind.[60]

While the Confederates were conducting their house to house search, the citizens began to emerge from their cellars and houses. They were naturally still dazed by it all as they began to assess the damage the fight through the streets had left on their town. The sights that greeted their eyes were cause for added shock and revulsion.

Alice Powers came out her front door and found the litter of savage fighting lying about High Street. There were several dead horses and dead men lying in the street and on the pavement right in front of her house. Up at the Methodist Church, adjoining the rear of the McCreary property, two more bodies were visible. One of these might have been the target of the shot that the McCrearys had heard following the order to, "..shoot that fellow going over the fence." Several doors to the east, in front of Salome Myers' house, an ammunition wagon stood abandoned.[61]

Sarah Broadhead, and her companions came out of their cellar only after nearby Confederates assured them that they would not be harmed. The destruction was all about them. Sarah described it in her diary: "The streets were strewn over with clothes, blankets, knapsacks, cartridge boxes, dead horses and the bodies of a few men..." After a brief assessment, she started back towards her house on Chambersburg Street where her husband Joseph had remained throughout the day.[62]

John Will confronted a similar scene as he attempted to venture north from the square along Carlisle Street with two companions, Dr. Goldsborough and Henry Stahle. Keeping to the middle of the street, they saw the scattered debris of equipment and, "..several dead men lying on the west side of the street..," between the 'Diamond' and the railroad tracks. The sights were overwhelming and before long he and his companions retraced their steps to the square. John returned to the Globe Inn and remained there for the evening.[63]

Jennie McCreary had earlier left her home in the first block of Chambersburg Street to help "roll bandages" with some other women at the house of a Mrs. Weaver. She was cut off from her house by the retreat through town. As the fighting in the center of town abated, she was able to venture out and return home. That short walk presented Jennie with a path of horrors: ". . a good many of our soldiers were killed in our street. I saw two dead ones lying in McCurdy's alley when I crossed the street to go home. Four of our men were carrying a wounded soldier on a stretcher down the street when a ball came along and took the legs off the two front men. There were some Rebels killed too."[64]

On the southern end of town the situation remained tense with the continued danger from the firing between combatants. The Confederates formed their advanced skirmish lines among the houses there, facing the Union skirmishers on the slope of Cemetery Hill. After beating back a Union reconnaissance launched at dusk between Baltimore and S. Washington Sts., the Rebels occupied houses and buildings in the area south from Breckenridge Street. Some houses, such as the Harvey Sweney home on Baltimore at South Street, were particularly exposed, forcing the occupants to evacuate for the duration. Confederates burst into the house and occupied the garret, using the widow to shoot at Cemetery Hill. Catherine Sweney and daughter Lizzie sought a more protected part of town with just the clothes on their backs. They found refuge with the Solomon Powers family on the N.E. corner of High and S. Washington Streets.[65]

Up on Cemetery Hill the circumstances for Elizabeth Thorn and family were equally traumatic. Mrs. Thorn lived in the gate house to Evergreen Cemetery, and in her husband's absence in the army, served as the caretaker. Living with her were her three young sons and her parents. When reserve units from the 11th Corps first arrived on Cemetery Hill in the morning, Elizabeth busied herself with baking bread which the soldiers, "..took out of my hands as fast as she could cut it..." During the early afternoon she actually led an officer on horseback, "..over East Cemetery Hill quite a distance..," to point out the roads running eastward from the town. The whole time she stayed on the southeast side of the mount to shield from stray missiles. The hurried arrival of the retreating Union forces later that afternoon replaced the earlier spectacle of distant battle with immediate danger from Confederate bullets and artillery shells. The Thorns took to their cellar. After dark, when the firing had subsided, Elizabeth was summoned upstairs to prepare a meal of pan cakes and a few scraps of meat for Union generals Howard, Slocum and Sickles. Around midnight she returned to her family and a few hours of fitful sleep. At dawn on July 2nd, General Howard would order the Thorns to vacate their house immediately to insure their safety. Elizabeth, her three boys and parents would leave with no possessions, and venture south along the Baltimore Pike toward Littlestown in search of a safe-haven. (66)

The rest of the town began to settle down for the coming night. The high energy level present all day among the troops and civilians now began to give way to exhaustion. The main Confederate battle line consisting of Rodes' and Early's Divisions were advanced into town and deployed along Middle and High Streets. That maneuver placed close to five thousand dirty, sweaty soldiers into a town with facilities to support a population of just one half that number. One can only speculate as to the degree the odors emitted from so many unwashed bodies deteriorated the atmosphere in the town.

The establishment of the battle line on the streets of Gettysburg brought the townspeople into a new level of contact with the Confederates, up close and personal. As soon as the initial uncertainty and fear passed, normal communications commenced between soldier and civilian. The initial dialogue was driven by the needs to satisfy creature comforts. Soldiers were tired and hungry and the bargaining for food with civilians began immediately. There was also the need for water and, of course, privy facilities. The local people were in no way equipped to deal with the level of demand, but in the case of food and water there is ample evidence in most reminiscences, that they did their best to share what they could.

It is striking that no mention is found anywhere as to how the body function needs of the Confederates were accommodated. To find the answer we must invoke our imagination. With minimum speculation we can arrive at an assumption that back yards became vast latrines, with attending odors adding to the already foul atmosphere being endured by the citizens.

The soldiers lay down along the pavements bordering the streets. Their attitude was one of joyous confidence based on the outcome of the day's fighting. Before drifting off to sleep many struck up conversations with their reluctant hosts. Leander Warren's father, David, engaged in a long conversation with a Confederate officer concerning the issues of the war. So pleasant was the dialogue that David and his wife invited the stranger to be their guest for supper.

William McClean ventured out on the crowded pavement in front of his house. He found the Confederates to be friendly enough. He was particularly relieved when they reacted in good humor to his six year old daughter Mary's impromptu rendition of 'Hang Jeff Davis on a Sour Apple Tree'.[67]

For a few there was no time to unwind and rest. The needs of the wounded would recognize no time clock. Dr. James Fulton, surgeon assigned to the 143rd PA., walked down from his hospital in the Catholic Church to the Myers residence and asked for the use of the cook stove. Spying the Myers girls he implored them to assist: "You must come up to the church and help us." Salome agreed to go and, "..from that time we had no rest for weeks." Her initial stay inside the church was brief. The horrible wounds and pitiful moans of the maimed, lying everywhere on the pews and on the floor, simply overwhelmed her senses. She turned and hurried out the door where she dissolved into a fit of uncontrollable sobbing. Upon regaining her composure, Salome went back into the church and unflinchingly went about the task of helping and comforting the suffering.[68]

Over on Baltimore Street, Agnes Barr turned her kitchen into a commissary to prepare food for the medical staff and patients at the nearby Presbyterian Church. It would prove to be an around the clock endeavor for days to come. Barr recalled that she was, ". . glad that we could do it." Gates Fahnestock's mother began non stop baking for the Union wounded being cared for in the courthouse. The next day more and more of Gettysburg's citizens would be required to labor for the needs of the wounded.[69]

At last it was time for all to give into their fatigue and seek sleep. Although exhausted from the emotional stress and the excitement of events, rest did not come easily to Gettysburg that night. Their town was occupied by the enemy. This was naturally a cause for some "despondency" and they went to bed, ". . not knowing what to expect on the morrow."[70] Alice Powers' recollection provided a fitting summary for the day: "At night all was quiet, but the tramp of the guards reminded the town that its citizens were prisoners."[71]

JULY 2nd: "O! how I dread tomorrow"

With those sentiments Sarah Broadhead began a fitful night of sleep. Shortly after midnight she was awake and at her front window. By the light of the moon she watched some Confederates systematically loot a house across the street whose owners had fled town the previous day. After loading up a wagon with their plunder they drove off. Sarah feared that they would return to burglarize her own house. She noted in her diary: "I expected every minute that they would burst in our door."[1] Fortunately her anxiety proved unwarranted.

Fear of plundering and looting by Confederates was a common concern among the citizens that first night. Mary McAllister was apprehensive even though she had procured a guard from the Christ Lutheran Church hospital detail who slept on her doorstep. Mary kept a personal vigil each night of the Confederate occupation by sleeping in a chair placed before a open bedroom window overlooking the street and her front door. She would lay her head on crossed arms that rested on the window sill and catch catnaps. Behind her slept her sister and four nephews and nieces, lying crosswise on a single bed. Space was at a premium with the house full of wounded. Like Sarah Broadhead, Mary's fears of vandalism on the part of Confederate renegades never materialized.[2]

Catherine Foster and her family were not quite as fortunate. Like so many others that first night, the Fosters had trouble sleeping. Much of the time Catherine spent at the window watching the firefly flashes of, "..the picket fighting." Just before daybreak they were awakened for good by a loud pounding on their back door. Two soldiers demanded to be let in to search for "Yankees." Knowing that Cpl. Wilcox was hiding in their basement led Catherine to try and dissuade the Confederates from their intent. Protests that the house had already been searched did not change their determination to enter the house. Concerned about what they might do to the house or its occupants if she resisted further, Catherine let them in. Once inside the two soldiers made no attempt to search the house, but right away pointed their guns at her father, James Foster, and demanded $50. Mr. Foster protested that he had nothing more than what was in his wallet. They took the wallet and left with only several dollars for their effort.[3]

This was one of a very few occasions of forced entry and robbing of citizens during the Confederate occupation of Gettysburg. While the Confederates did routinely enter and ransack unoccupied houses, they did not normally enter and rob people who remained with their homes.

The Moses McClean family also had a nocturnal experience that was unsettling, but short of robbery. Soon after midnight, "..we were all aroused by a loud rapping on the door." Moses leaned out of a upstairs window and inquired as to what was wanted. The response was that General Ramseur had sent them to confiscate a supply of bacon. When Moses protested that his was a private home and that he did not keep supplies, the Confederate officer threatened to enter by force. Fearing possible harm to his family, McClean yielded. The Confederates were led back through the yard to the smoke house. The hams were gathered up and the party returned to the house. By the light of an oil lamp the officer wrote out a receipt, handing it to McClean with the comment: "..your government ought to pay you for that." Lizzie, the McClean's live-in domestic, brazenly replied: "..our government would have a great deal to pay for all you steal." Without further comment the Confederates departed with their requisitioned breakfast. [4]

For the majority of citizens there were no incidents with their captors during the night. The initial impression of the new day was described by Daniel Skelly in his recollections: "Day dawned bright and clear. We did not know what to expect ...but we were soon assured, that with certain restrictions, we could go about town." [5] This was not to say that life in the town was normal. Things were terribly different. Crowds of soldiers were awakening and beginning to light cook fires along the pavements of Middle Street and to seek facilities for their morning toiletries and necessaries.

As the town began its first full day under Confederate occupation, the frantic and violent pace of events of the evening before were replaced with a tense calm. The two armies, both swollen in numbers from the arrival of reenforcements, faced each other in almost silent anticipation. Each were engaged in activities to strengthen their respective positions. In the town, the Confederates erected barricades in the streets and alleys to present obstacles to any possible attack launched from Cemetery Hill. The stone wall running along the south side of W. Middle Street was redirected across S. Washington Street. Barricades of various materials were erected across Baltimore Street at Breckenridge, and the alleys running north and south. To facilitate troop movement in the town many of the yard fences were dismantled. Some of the material was undoubtedly used in the construction of the barricades. Out on the far western end of Middle Street an entire log house was dismantled and used for fortifications. [6] The destruction of property by the Confederates to turn Gettysburg into a fortress far exceeded actual battle damage.

The preparations by the Confederates sent a message to the civilians that the early morning calm was only temporary and anxieties began to rise. David Warren was moved to action. His house sat along Railroad Street on the south side of the tracks, half way between Carlisle and N. Washington Streets. Immediately upon arising he woke Leander, and they went out and pushed a rail car loaded with lime along the track into position in front of the house. The idea was to shield the basement and first floor windows from stray bullets. Warren's intentions were sound, but he was closing the stable door after the horse had fled. His house faced north. The battle lines were now to the south. To make matters worse the Confederates tearing down his fences warned that the Yankees would soon shell the town. That was enough for the Warrens. The family made quick preparations to leave town. Upon emerging from their house an officer advised that if they left their house it would surely be ransacked and they could loose everything. Considering the options, they decided to risk the Yankee shells. The forecasted shelling never came, but another hazard took its place. Sometime during the morning, soldiers broke into the cellar of the Washington Hotel at the corner of Carlisle and Railroad Streets and confiscated whiskey. In a short time they were drunk and several turned ugly, "..making it real hot for every person around."[7]

All around the town people were trying to go about their lives while adjusting to the presence of the war and an occupying army. At the Globe Inn there was an early management crisis. A large group of Confederate officers gathered at the door and inquired if they could be served breakfast. They were told they could and were placed as a group at a long, common table which accommodated forty six at a seating. The Will's were opportunistic entrepreneurs. They arbitrarily raised their prices by fifty percent. No bother to their famished customers who enthusiastically dug into the meal. Then came the real test, collection of the bill. Charles told his son to refuse Confederate currency and accept only "good money" or close the dinning room. This was a situation that could be explosive and it was a apprehensive John Will that rendered the tab. To his great relief the Confederates paid in "green backs," some even offering gold. The source of such currency was never established, but since the officers were from Early's command it was surmised that the money was part of the ransom extorted from the city of York, several days earlier. For the Will's the profit opportunity looked grand. They readily welcomed back their Confederate guests for every meal during their stay in town.[8]

Even though the Confederates did not confine them to their homes, many citizens were reluctant to venture out into the streets. Robert McClean reported that his family spent the duration of the occupation in their house, other than a few excursions to and from his brother William's house. Charles McCurdy recalled his family did the same. Fannie Buehler was fearful of the possible dangers from random missiles and never left the protection of her brick walls. Mary Horner remembered: "..there was very little gadding about during those three days. Occasionally we ventured to the hospital (in the Christ Lutheran Church) or to get milk."[9]

When a person did venture out the experience was apt not to be very pleasant. William McClean's wife Fannie woke up in the morning feeling ill. Her husband was determined to consult the family doctor for medicine. His physician, Dr. Henry A. Huber lived two and one half blocks away. William found the trip to be a little unsettling: "I wended my way through the Rebel line of battle on Middle Street and by S. Washington Street to Chambersburg Street, to Dr. Huber... I had the old unfriendly eyes of the Rebel soldiery upon me as I passed through their ranks. There were little puddles of blood here and there...Gettysburg never presented such a ragged and forbidding appearance before or since."[10]

Mary McAllister also encountered dismal sights that morning when she went out searching for milk to serve the wounded in her house. She walked down Chambersburg Street to the Alexander Cobean property, directly across Washington Street from Dr. Huber's. In the small barn to the rear, she found a cow already milked, but was able to coax a half bucket. Her return trip was side tracked by the residue of yesterday's fighting through town. As a result she gave up most of the fruit of her labors by the time she returned home. As Mary recalled: "Just at the gate (to Cobean's yard) lay a dead man and there were wounded on the pavement. "Oh," they said, "give us some milk"..I returned with hardly a pint."[11]

Hannah McClean left the safety of her house to go help son William with his sick wife. On her way up Baltimore Street to Middle Street she came upon the body of a dead horse, killed the day before. The carcass was already swelling and in the July heat would soon be a source of putrid odor. Upon her return she notified her husband of the dead horse. Moses McClean went with fellow attorney, Robert McCreary, to see General Ewell about removing the horse. Ewell was sympathetic, but declined to help with the explanation: "..he had more important business on hand just then than burying dead horses."[12]

John Will had a similar problem at the Globe Inn. A dead horse was lying in the street before their front door. John and a friend approached a Confederate officer about removing the horse, even offering to pay. The officer's reply dripped with his contempt: "You people up here are very nice. Why didn't your men help us take away the dead from our doors at Fredericksburg?" With that he turned and rode off.[13]

With very few exceptions the Confederates kept to their promise not to molest the townspeople. On the other hand they knew that they were masters of the situation and they used that fact to bully and intimidate citizens into complying with their wishes. Nellie Aughinbaugh left a good example of such an occasion in her recollections. The townspeople were providing volunteer nurses to assist with the overwhelming number of wounded, but there was still the issue of procuring and preparing food for many of the hospitals. According to Nellie: "The Confederates.. ordered townspeople to make coffee and ginger bread to send to the hospitals." The local bakeries were drafted into this effort. Some, like Valentine Sauppee's on York Street, worked their ovens around the clock. Mrs. James Fahnestock baked continually for the wounded in the courthouse. Fannie Buehler spared food, prepared for the wounded in her care, for the courthouse. Undoubtedly many others not mentioned in personal reminiscences were drafted or even forced into this humanitarian effort.[14]

Beginning at daybreak, food became a source of contention between the occupying soldiers and the general population. Supplies were limited for both parties, naturally leading to some confrontations. The soldiers search for food sources were unrelenting. Nellie Aughinbaugh remembered seeing hungry soldiers, while in the act of ransacking her uncle's store, ". . knock the tops from kegs of salt mackerel, snatch the fish from the brine and eat them, heads, tails and all." At the Jacob Hollinger household, there were repeated requests by the Confederates for their cow. Each time they were refused with the excuse that she, "..was too old." Some came and wanted to feed the green garden corn to their horses. This request was also turned down. A third party arrived and demanded the keys to Mr. Hollinger's warehouse where feed and molasses were stored. Again Hollinger refused with the statement: "I can not prevent it, but I am not inviting you by giving you the keys." The Confederates got the point and went back to break through the locked doors, taking their fill and spoiling what they left.[15]

Food for many of the families was tight and sharing with an insatiable enemy would have jeopardized their own survival. Mary Montfort recalled their near desperate situation years later when writing her recollections: "We didn't have much food in the house. We ate a little fish each day and for our other meals we would eat biscuits and pancakes with apple butter." The biscuits and pancakes were made possible as a result of a clever trick by a neighbor to keep his cow from Confederate hands and mess kits. Lem Snyder brought the Montfort's a pail of milk, essential for baking. When asked how come the Confederates did not take his cow, Lem explained: "I took 'Bessie' and tied her in the parlor. She's been there since. Now we have milk to share with our neighbors."[16]

At the Solomon Powers house, Catherine Powers likewise used a little deceit to preserve the family food source. Several soldiers were seen coming into the backyard intent on capturing the family laying hens, then roosting in the peach trees. Thinking quickly, Mrs Powers turned adversity into good fortune by admonishing the soldiers in their endeavor, since the chickens were intended, she claimed, "..for the poor wounded southerners in her house" (the wounded cared for by the Powers ladies were Union boys). The hunters quickly backed off their game and even helped Mrs. Powers round the chickens up and put them in the hen house.[17] It is not known what they found to substitute for their almost chicken dinner.

The truce between citizen and soldier was tenuous at best and obviously not founded on a deep trust. Mistrust cost at least two hungry Confederates a much needed meal. The two approached the Scott house begging for food. Martha fetched a newly baked pie and placed it before them. The immediate acquiescence to their request must have raised suspicion. They refused to eat it in fear that it might be poisoned.

"You eat a piece," came the demand.

Mary McAllister responded: "Do you think it is poisoned? The women here don't poison food."

Despite this reassurance, the skeptical Confederates were unconvinced and left as they arrived, hungry.[18]

It is hard to judge who won this tug of war over food. In the short run it could be called a draw. The combined demands exhausted the supply by the end of the Confederate stay, but nobody went entirely without. The town would suffer the most in the longer term, the coming winter. Charles McCurdy offered a accurate assessment in his recollections: "I do not know the fate of numerous pigs and cows on which many families were dependent for winter meat. Doubtless they helped to supply the scanty commissary of the enemy." Unfortunately the same applied to the many kitchen gardens wiped out by hungry Confederates. These not only supplied summer vegetables but supplied the dry cellar larders for winter. Alice Powers bemoaned the plight of the gardens: " No wonder hands were wrung and tears flowed at the dismal sights (of destruction) for many depended in great measure on these large gardens for a living."[19]

As the day wore on other irritants grew from the situation which became cause for annoyance and anxiety among the townspeople. The gas house was shut down, leaving many people without a source of light in their homes. This increased fears as nightfall approached. And there was the frustration and sense of helplessness of being cut off from all communication with the outside world. Daniel Skelly recalled: "We knew nothing about our army. The Confederates maintained a clam like silence on all matters concerning the battle."[20]

While the citizens in the center of town busied themselves with the trials of co-existence with an occupying army, the people still remaining with their homes in the southern portion of town faced an all together different set of circumstances. They were caught between the hostile skirmish lines. With the first light of dawn the firing between opposing sharpshooters opened in earnest. Wherever possible the combatants fortified themselves in houses and fired from doorways and windows. Some of the houses had been vacated, others had not. The Confederates had the advantage along Baltimore, Washington and Breckenridge Streets because their lines encompassed the more developed area and they had more houses available for their protection. In this neighborhood the proximity of opposing lines was close.

At the John Rupp tannery on Baltimore Street, the advanced elements of each skirmish line actually occupied opposite sides of the Rupp house. Rupp spent the duration between them, huddled in his basement: "The Rebs occupied the whole of town out as far as the back end of my house...Our men occupied my porch, and the Rebel(s) the rear of the house, and I in the cellar, so you can see I was on neutral ground." His situation was not a passive standoff. Describing his experience after the battle he noted: "I could hear the Rebs load their guns and fire. There was one of our men killed under my big oak tree.. I gathered up a double handful of `minie' balls in my dwelling...that were shot into it from both armies."[21] The nearness of the lines at Rupp's was an exception. As a norm, most of the dueling between sharpshooters took place at ranges from 200 to 400 yards.

The families that were trapped in their homes were forced to spend much of the daylight hours in their cellars. Even at night some took cautious measures. At the Garlach house, the family had spent the night on the bedroom floors in fear, "..bullets would come in the windows and reach us." Before day break Catherine Garlach and her twelve year old son Will set about making their cellar habitable despite the foot or so of rain water. It would be impossible for them to go up the street to a neighbor's to seek shelter with the Federal soldiers firing at any sign of movement in the area. They carried logs stored in the backyard for making chair rungs into the cellar and stood them on end so as to protrude above the standing water. Catherine then connected the up-turned logs with boards creating a makeshift floor. It was a safe fortress. Neighbors, with less secure quarters or forced to abandon their homes to the soldiers, "drifted in" until eleven persons in addition to the four Garlachs shared the safety of the cellar. Catherine organized the seating by family groups, and: "..each party knew the place he or she was to occupy."[22]

While the exchange of shots was constant throughout the day the intensity varied. During the slack periods people could come out of their cellars, but not out of their houses. At the Garlachs, Anna recalled: "We stayed in the kitchen most of the time except when there was firing, then we would go to our places in the cellar." During these interludes from the basement Anna managed: "..an occasional peep out of the windows." From the front room she watched a strange drama played out between some Confederates in the Winebrenner alley across the street and Union sharpshooters beyond her view on Cemetery Hill: "The building along the alley was brick and the men there had thrown up a kind of barricade on the pavement." While crouched out of sight they would: "..put a hat on a stick over the barricade and draw the fire of the Union sharpshooters." When the smoke revealed the location of the enemy riflemen, the Confederates would: "jump up and fire out the street."[23]

Several times Confederates tried to commandeer the Garlach house for a sharpshooter's lair. Each time Mrs. Garlach refused their request. On one occasion a Rebel marksman entered the front door uninvited, and started up the stairs to find a vantage point from which to fire on the Union troops. Hearing him start up the stairs, Catherine ran after him and caught his coat tail protesting: "You can't go up there. You will draw the fire on this house full of defenseless women and children." When the soldier said that he would surely be killed if he tried to leave, he was invited to stay, but he, "..must not fire from the house." After pausing to reflect on the proposal, the soldier decided he could better face the Yankees than he could deal with the resolve of Catherine Garlach. He went down the stairs, threw open the front door and discharged his rifle to create a smoke screen. Then, "..he darted out and got safely across the street into Winebrenner's alley."[24]

Despite Catherine Garlach's heroic efforts her house was still hit repeatedly. Confederates were using the garrets in Sweney house just to the front and the George Schriver house just beyond the Garlach's. Errant shots directed toward those targets often hit the Garlach house. There was one notable exception. The curiosity and persistence of young Will finally overcame the better judgement of Catherine and the result was almost fatal. During one of the afternoon's lulls, Will and Catherine went up into their garret to get a better look at the fighting from the small, south-end window. They removed the board sash and took a brief look toward Union positions on Cemetery Hill. Nothing much was going on and Catherine was nervous about being exposed, so they returned the cover board and turned to leave the garret. Only seconds after replacing the cover, and just when they started down the steps, a bullet tore through the left window jamb and entered the garret. Their brief appearance at the opening had drawn the attention of a Federal marksman and suspecting the presence of a Confederate, he had fired.[25]

Baltimore St. Looking north from Cemetery Hill. Wagon Hotel on the left. (USMHI)

In nearby houses the situation was even hotter. M.L. Culler, a student at the Lutheran Seminary, had taken refuge with the John Winebrenner family in their brick house, "..where the big Sycamore trees stood." Culler recalled that the Confederates, "..entered the house and discharged shots from the doors and windows." In addition, "..they took away everything edible except a small piece of dried beef and some coffee." Throughout the two day ordeal Culler and his hosts were forced to spend all the daylight hours in the cellar. From "their prison" the sounds of the battle above were clearly audible. The cannonading, "..caused the house to shake.." and the sounds of the, "..minie balls crashing through the windows and doors above us.." went on incessantly. The monotony and horror of the experience was broken by a brief interlude of a most unusual and civil gesture. After nightfall on July 3rd, a group of Confederates appeared at the side door and invited the occupants to be their guests for supper. Culler remembered: "..we were amazed at their proposal.." and sat down to enjoy an ample meal, "..for which I shall always cherish a feeling of gratitude."[26]

For a few, the spectacle of violence accompanied the frightening sounds of battle raging around them. In the Samuel McCreary house, just south of the Winebrenner building, the family was exposed to the horror of violent death. Louisianna troops were manning the Confederate skirmish line on the east side of Baltimore Street. One, Cpl. William H. Poole of the 9th LA., gained access to the McCreary house and went up to the 2nd floor to snipe at Federal riflemen located in the Wagon Hotel just a 100 yards away. Cpl. Poole got careless and it cost him his life. Wanting a better advantage from which to fire, he dragged a drop leaf table into the doorway that opened onto the balcony on the south side of the house. Kneeling behind the table he steadied his rifle on the top and continued with his deadly business. His position was clearly visible to his opponents and one sent a ball that crashed through the hanging table leaf and struck Poole in the chest, killing him instantly. In what must have been numbing shock, the McCreary family was left with the gruesome task of wiping up the fresh blood, wrapping Poole's body in a shroud of a family blanket and later burying his body nearby.[27]

The danger from stray and aimed sharpshooters bullets was not confined to the southern extremities of town. Federal marksmen posted well up the northern slope of Cemetery Hill could see beyond the crest of Baltimore Street hill and into the center of town. The range was extreme but that did not deter the marksmen. They let fire at any visible target. At that distance of 800 to 1000 yards they could not distinguish between soldier and civilian. People quickly learned to stay off of Baltimore Street, beyond High Street.

The David McCreary house being located at the intersection of Baltimore and High Streets provided the family members a real exposure to this deadly menace.

Albertus recalled that the missiles came with such frequency across the back yard that, "..none of us dared to go out to our barn." The situation was no different on the front or Baltimore Street side of the house, "..where we dared not look out of the windows." The only place the family could safely emerge from their house to get a breath of fresh air was on the High Street side, "..where we could stay out on the porch." Even this safe haven and the ability to get a respite from the confines of the house and cellar did not provide relief from the tension: "The sharp snap of bullets through the trees in the yard kept us well keyed up."[28]

he experience of William McClean with the sharpshooter menace was a lot more personal than that at the McCreary household. After taking the medicine prescribed by Dr. Huber, Fannie McClean began to feel better. With her mother-in-law present to care for the baby, she left her bed and retired with the rest of the family to the cellar. The confinement of the cellar, coupled with a nagging curiosity, worked to make William restless. Finally, he gave in and excused himself from the cellar to go up into the house. He went into the upstairs bedroom that his wife had just vacated and opened a front window shutter just, "..slightly to take a little look around." There was really not much to see and after a short time he turned away. The window had exposed him to the ever present danger of an errant missile. He had barely removed himself from in front of the window, "..when a minie ball came crashing through the shutter and sash." The bullet traveled, "..on a line of where my breast had been a few seconds before, entered the foot board of the bed in which my sick wife had been and passed into the mattress." A shaken William quickly returned to the cellar.[29]

This near miss was not an isolated incident. Salome Myers had a similar experience in her house. A mortally wounded and suffering Federal soldier had been removed from the Catholic Church to the Myers home to live out his last hours in as much comfort as could be afforded him. He was Sgt. Alexander Stewart, 149th PA.. Salome had been sitting for some time by his bed fanning away the uncomfortable heat. At last her cramping muscles got the better of her and she stood up from her stool to walk about and stretch. Immediately after rising, "..a minie ball came through two walls and struck the floor where I had been sitting a minute before. I would have been struck in the neck." Fate was not through smiling on Salome. Four days later Sgt. Stewart died. Soon after the battle ended his brother Henry visited to convey his appreciation to the Myers' for all their kindness. Following the end of the war Henry Stewart and Salome Myers, brought together by the battle and the death of Alexander Stewart, were married.[30]

Over on the east end of town the situation was no better. The Hollinger's house and yard were fully exposed to a wheat field beyond the Culp farm buildings in which a Federal skirmish line had deployed. They kept up a lively exchange of fire with their Confederate counterparts positioned closer to the town. Being in the line of this fire the Hollingers took to the safety of their cellar. From there they could hear the bullets, "..strike the brick walls of the house." But chores still needed to be done. When Jacob Hollinger ventured out to his barn to feed the chickens and cow the rate of fire intensified and focused on him. Narrowly escaping injury or worse, Hollinger got back to the lee side of the house. When he commented to a nearby Confederate officer about the Federal skirmishers seeming to deliberately shoot at him, he got some sound advice: "Why man, take off that gray suit. They think you are a Reb." The advice was heeded.[31]

About 4P.M. the war returned in earnest for the citizens of Gettysburg. The occasion was marked by the opening of heavy artillery fire all along the opposing lines. Once again shells went screeching over the town. This time the people did not have to be told to take to their cellars. In an instant the streets were empty of civilians. There were exceptions. The lingering curiosity to see as well as hear the action almost proved costly to a few.

The Globe Inn in the 1st block of York St. ca. 1862 (ACHS)

John Will climbed to the roof of the Globe Inn and was watching the deployment of Latimer's Confederate battery on Benner's Hill to the east of town. In a few minutes he heard a shout, "..get off that roof!" Glancing about he saw no one and continued with his vigil. Again, and then again, the call came to get off the roof. This time Will saw a Confederate soldier, a block away to the south on E. Middle St., with his rifle pointed at him. John inquired of the fellow as to: "..who he was talking to?"

The soldier replied: "I am talking to you and I want you to get off that roof."

John became stubborn and merely changed his position so as to be screened from the soldier's view by the chimney. A minute later a Confederate officer appeared at the rear of the Inn on horseback with his revolver in hand. The stalemate had become tense. The officer announced: "General Early wants to see you and if you come down now you shall not be hurt." Seeing that his mother and two sisters were, "..very much frightened," Will acquiesced. Accompanied by the officer and several others from the hotel, John was marched to Early's headquarters at the John Cannon marble works on E. Middle Street. There he was subjected to a heated lecture on the follies of a recalcitrant civilian population. Early was clearly angry. He knew that the presence of the two armies exposed the town to considerable danger and he felt responsible for the citizens' safety.

"What were you doing on the roof?", he demanded.

"I was looking over the battle," was John's reply.

Early fairly exploded: "Your people are on the streets. They are at their garret windows. I sent guards door to door to tell them to get into their cellars or at least stay inside, the only safe place. I want to save your people."

Getting his frustrations out evidently calmed the General. John was not arrested and he returned to the Inn and stayed inside.[32]

At about the same time, and a block to the west, Henry Jacobs and his father were exhibiting the type of behavior that was trying General Early's patience. At Michael's suggestion they decided to leave the cellar and go out into the back yard to better "..hear the cannonade." Emerging, they sat down on their, "..old-fashioned sloping cellar door." They were there but a short time when the noise of battle added a new pitch. Musketry now could be heard intermingled with the dull thud of exploding artillery shells. In an instant bullets began to fall about them. The obvious danger from the flying mini balls, ". . made us retreat hastily to the refuge of the cellar," closing the entrance doors behind them. A nearby soldier, one of Dole's Georgians, took their place sitting on the cellar door. He suffered a tragic end which the Jacobs' just barely avoided. Henry recalled the awful moment when the stray bullet struck: "He suddenly groaned and we heard his body fall over and gently slide downward."[33]

A half block to the east of the Jacobs' on W. Middle St., the Harvey Wattles family and several neighbors were sitting out the cannonade in the Wattles' spacious cellar. Daniel Skelly and his family were there. They all passed the storm in safety and that night, when the shelling had ceased, they emerged to a stark reminder of the violence they had avoided. Skelly remembered the incident: "A neighbor had come into the house to take refuge and had brought a band box containing a bonnet. When fleeing into the cellar she left the box on the chair upon which she had been sitting. When she came up...she found the box with a mini ball having passed through the box and the bonnet."[34]

Misdirected artillery shells joined mini balls in falling into the town. Gettysburg itself was never a deliberate target for artillery shelling by either side (with the exception of one or two buildings infested with Confederate sharpshooters) despite several warnings to the contrary. There were occasions on all three days of battle when shells were hurled back and forth over the town. When this happened there were incidents in which buildings in the town were struck due to defective shells or poor aim. Fortunately no one was killed or even seriously wounded by these accidents. There were, however, some close calls and scary moments.

George Little and his wife lived in a two story brick house just a few houses west of Daniel Skelly. The Littles were joined by eight others, women and children, from the neighborhood, and all were sitting in a small room at the rear of the house. Soon after the bombardment began two shells exploded in the yard just a short distance away. The result was fright and panic among the refugees in the room. Why they did not retire immediately to the cellar is not known for certain. Most probably it was because the cellar entrance was external to the house and in the yard just struck by the shells. Instead they remained in the room trembling, when one of the girls asked: "Oh, what shall we do?"

"Pray," was the response from George Little.

At that instant a third shell struck nearer to the door. That was enough. Braving the danger, Little led his flock out into the yard and then down into the cellar. Almost before they had descended into the basement a shrapnel shell struck the rear door jamb and entered the room they had just vacated. The shell exploded, destroying everything within. Providence had spared all ten from almost certain death.[35]

On the southern end of Baltimore Street, a young girl had the worst fright of her life when a shell entered the room in which she was standing. Laura Bergstresser, the young daughter of the Methodist minister, was standing near the window in the upstairs front room of their brick home. While she was there a shell struck the wall just to the left of the window, entered the room without exploding and miraculously ricocheted around the room and passed out through the window without harming Laura. In fact she suffered nothing more than a bout of hysteria which was soon quelled. It was another case of Divine Providence intervening to prevent certain tragedy.[36]

Mary McAllister was once again out and about despite the danger flying overhead. This time her quest was for liquor rather than milk. Several of the Federal officers convalescing in the Scott house were begging for some stronger medicine than the tea and water prescribed by the surgeons. Finally Mary acquiesced to their pleas and headed out with a empty canteen. She went down the block several buildings to Buehler's Drug Store where liquor for medicinal purposes could be purchased. While Mr. Buehler was filling the canteen, "..a shell burst through the front door," but did not explode. Both Mary and Buehler were badly shaken. Mary was hesitant about going back on to the street. The druggist handed over the canteen and urged Mary to quickly be on her way: "Well, you will be killed if you stay." As she passed through what had been the front door, he admonished her: "Don't let them (Rebels) see it." She made it home with her "medicine" without detection or injury. It was just what the doctor ordered for lagging spirits. The officers took the whiskey, ",,and I can tell you it brought song." It also nearly cost Mary McAllister her life.[37]

Sarah Broadhead's family, the Jacob Gilberts and the other two families of 'Warren's Row' on Chambersburg Street all gathered in the cellar of David Troxel's house, which was set back from the pavement along the west side of the Broadheads. Elizabeth Gilbert recorded: "They were pretty well crowded." In fact there were twenty two people in the cellar and the anxiety was high, with everyone trying to "..keep up each other's courage." At some point a shell entered the upper floor of the house, but did not explode. Both Elizabeth Gilbert and Sarah Broadhead mentioned the incident in their memoirs. The reaction among everyone in the cellar was denial. Elizabeth wrote that the impact was clearly detectable in the basement, but no one mentioned it out of fear that, "..it would excite the women and children."[38]

About 5 o'clock a horse and wagon pulled up beside the John Burns house. The wagon contained the family of Anthony Sellinger and the wounded John Burns. The Sellingers, next door neighbors of Burns, had left their house early that morning to avoid a rumored shelling of the town by Union artillery. Returning along the Chambersburg Pike they were stopped on Seminary Ridge by Confederate soldiers who asked them to carry a wounded civilian into town. The soldiers went into the small stone house beside the road and brought out John Burns, suffering from wounds, but walking with support. The Confederates did not realize that Burns had been an enemy combatant. They told Anthony that the old man had told them he had been, "..out to buy some chickens when he got shot." Burns was laid in the wagon bed in the company of the two children. Ten year old Michael Sellinger was traumatized by the sight of his neighbor's bloody trousers and frequent moaning during the 1/2 mile trip into town. Once there Anthony and, "..some other man..," helped Burns into his house and the care of his wife.[39]

As darkness fell the artillery fire subsided and people emerged from their shelters. The respite from the din of battle was short. Before it was fully dark, two brigades of Early's Division launched an attack on the east side of Cemetery Hill from their position in the southeast outskirts of the town. The fighting was just a half mile from the center of town, and the noise of the combat, in the memory of Henry Jacobs, "..was actually deafening". Albertus McCreary described it, "..as if a millon boys with sticks were beating on a board fence." For Fannie Buehler, "..it was the most awful time of the awful battle...the ground trembled, on which our house stood." For the second time that day, the fear of deadly missiles falling on their heads sent the town's civilian population scurrying into their cellars.[40]

One exception was the household of Agnes Barr. Even though her house was particularly exposed on top of Baltimore Street hill, she and her sisters kept to their task of preparing food for the surgeons and patients at the Presbyterian Church. During the height of the action on Cemetery Hill several Union doctors were seated at her kitchen table. Some Confederates, from the reserve line resting in the adjacent alley, spotted them through the window and curtly inquired of Barr as to why she was feeding Yankees. When informed that they were doctors serving the wounded at the church, their hostile attitude vanished. They even refused an invitation to share the meal, "..insisting that it all go to the wounded."[41]

Like the Barr's, the Scott household was also too busy with a crisis to drop everything and go to cover. The condition of a patient, with a bullet still embedded in his back, was beginning to worsen. While Martha wiped his brow, her sister Mary McAllister went to find a surgeon. She went first to Belle King's house next door, where several doctors were attending wounded. She explained that the bullet was clearly visible under the skin and would not be difficult to remove. Her pleas for help were ignored and she was dismissed with, "..some sass." She retraced her steps and went to another neighbor, Dr. Robert Horner. He agreed to take a look. The situation was made more difficult by the lack of light. The town's gas was turned off and the Scott's evidently had no oil lamps for emergencies. Martha improvised by dipping some twisted paper in lard to create a crude candle. It worked. Dr. Horner popped the bullet out and gave it to the patient saying: "There, take that and put it in your knapsack for a keepsake."

The man smiled weakly and replied: "I feel better already."[42]

The excitement at the Scott's was not over for the evening. Shortly after Dr. Horner left, two Confederate soldiers came to the door and said that they would guard the house. Instead of guarding the door, they entered the house and began taunting the patients. Mary ordered them out, but they refused to leave and became "sassy." At that moment an officer came down the street and Mary rushed out with an appeal for help in getting the intruders to leave. The officer quickly resolved the situation and was rewarded with a supper meal by lard light.[43]

By ten o'clock the battlefield had fallen silent with the exception of the ever present picket fire. The townspeople began to settle down for their second night under Confederate occupation. They had adjusted to their situation remarkably well and were no longer in a state of high anxiety and fear. The lack of news as to what was going on was still unsettling. Gates Fahnestock remembered vividly years later: "It was an anxious time with us. We had no news of how the battle was going." And the Confederates were not talking, at least not on E. Middle Street. William McClean, who lived just a few houses east of the Fahnestock's, had much the same experience. He tried to be friendly and gain their confidence. He gave a dose of Aver's Wild Cherry Pectoral to an officer who complained of a sore throat. He mingled with the troops in front of his house who had just returned from the assault on Cemetery Hill. Despite his generosity and affability he got little or no information from any of them. They were only communicative enough to inquire as to, "..the road and distance to Baltimore." Apparently Confederate reticence regarding the status of the conflict varied by unit. Two blocks away, at the Foster's house, they were very accommodating. According to Catherine Foster: "The Rebels always appraised us of the hours and places fighting would be resumed. This gave us some comfort."[44]

Even though they had grown somewhat accustomed to the presence of the Confederates in town, most people still felt some apprehension about the dangers of stray bullets interrupting their sleep. The protective measures taken by the Moses McClean household can be assumed to be representative of many in town as they settled down to sleep that night. In her memoirs Elizabeth described the sleeping arrangements: "The boys..laid down on the floor below the window so no stray bullets could hit them. My sister Sallie and I..lay down on the floor also."[45]

Whatever the sleeping arrangements, it would prove to be a short night for all.

JULY 3RD: "..it seemed as if the Heavens and Earth were crashing together"

This was how Sarah Broadhead remembered the fighting around Gettysburg that day. It began at approximately 4 A.M. with a, "..fierce cannonading." This was the opening of a seven hour struggle for Culp's Hill. Almost instantly David Troxel's cellar was filled with the familiar refugees from 'Warren's Row'.[1] Many, but not everyone, in town followed that course of action and in several cases the lack of caution nearly cost the principals their lives.

At Catherine Foster's, the family immediately headed for the cellar. Two Union army surgeons remained in their bedroom on the 2nd floor. They were overnight guests of the Fosters, who were working in the nearby hospitals. Even though they were prisoners of war, they had the freedom to move about the town due to the nature of their work with the wounded. Befriending the Fosters, they were invited to quarter there. In deference to their state of near exhaustion, the Fosters did not disturb them when they went to the cellar shortly before dawn. Around 6 A.M. Catherine could no longer stand it and went to wake them. They were already up and quickly came down for a brief breakfast and left. Not five minutes after they departed a shell came through the side of the house into the room they had occupied: "..sending the (fireplace) mantle across the room and demolishing everything before it, tearing every particle of bedding from the bed on which they had lain." This shell was followed shortly by another which entered the breakfast room and, "..burst over the table," where only moments before both the family and their guests were seated. Fortunately the family members were going down the cellar stairs when the shell arrived. This was the third strike from artillery fire suffered by the Foster's house in three days. It would be the last, but it left the building with the dubious distinction of suffering the most artillery hits of any house in the town.[2]

Several blocks away, in the Moses McLean house, a similar situation occurred, involving a misguided artillery shell. The family was awakened early by the resumption of the fighting on Culp's Hill. Unlike the Foster's, the McCleans decided it was unnecessary to go to the cellar. The action seemed to be rather remote. Mrs. McClean went about some chores, choosing to haul a feather mattress upstairs to the garret for storage until cooler weather returned. She went up and cleared a space and returned to the 2nd floor to solicit the help of one of her sons to carry the mattress up the garret steps. While she was waiting, "..there was a loud crash and a shell came tearing through a 15 inch brick wall..," splitting a roof joist and then breaking an old crib. Then it, "..rolled down the stairs to the first landing," near where Hannah McClean she was standing. The dust in the garret was so thick that at first it was mistaken for smoke, "..but the shell did not explode." Once again, by the Grace of Providence, no one was hurt. When the wall was repaired a shell was mortared into the external side to mark the place of entry. The one that actually hit the house was kept by the family as a grim memento of those terrifying days.[3]

About the time the McCleans were facing their ordeal by fire, Gettysburg's most significant human tragedy of the battle was taking place. At the Louis and Georgia McClellan house on Baltimore Street, half way up the north slope of Cemetery Hill, Providence finally turned her back on the people of Gettysburg. The one and a half story brick house stood in the midst of the Federal skirmish line. Since the late afternoon of July 1st, the troops around the house carried on a deadly game of sniping with their Confederate adversaries, mainly around the Rupp Tannery buildings a 150 yards to the north. When the daylight was sufficient to see on the morning of the 3rd, the contest was renewed. Bullets began to strike the McClellan house, some entering the north side windows. Inside the house Georgia McClellan lay in bed with her new born son. Her younger sister, Jennie Wade, was in the kitchen to the rear of the house preparing dough for biscuits. Jennie's mother Mary was in the room with her, tending the fire. With a loud crash a bullet ripped through the outside door in the north side of the house, passed through a panel of an inside door and struck Jennie full in the back. The bullet retained enough force to pass completely through her body, piercing her heart on its way. In that instant Jennie transformed from a ordinary, mortal being into immortality. Her passage was not heralded by trumpets. Her mother announced the dreadful news in a manner perfectly fitting for one understandably in a state of shock. With very little show of outward emotion, she walked the few feet to the front parlor and simply stated: "Georgia, your sister is dead."[4] Gettysburg had suffered its' only civilian fatality of the battle.

There is a strong possibility that another civilian fatality was intended. John Burns, the ancient citizen who went out to resist the Confederate advance on July 1st and was wounded three times, claimed he was the targeted victim. According to Burns, he was convalescing in his home at the foot of Chambersburg Street when two Confederate officers arrived to question him about his alleged role in the fighting in McPherson's woods. Up until the morning of July 3rd, the Confederates had not suspected that he had fought against them. The day before, Burn's wounds had been treated by a Confederate surgeon and he had received, "..decent treatment until a 'Copperhead' woman living opposite, told on him." After some hard questioning, in which he gave them "..little satisfaction..," the officers left. In a few minutes two shots rang out from close by and Burns' house was struck. Both bullets entered through the same window. One passed a little high, over Burns' head and, "..struck the wall behind the lounge on which he was lying." The other one was, "..low, passing through a door." Burns steadfastly maintained that the shots were not random and were designed to, "..assassinate him."[5]

By mid morning the fighting on Culp's Hill subsided and citizens turned to another day of living with the enemy. There were few surprises this day. They had pretty well learned what to expect from their enemy hosts the day before. The attitude of the Confederates toward them was not hostile, but business like. Food was still a major focus and the town's gardens continued to suffer from the scavenging of the hungry soldiers.

Houses and their contents, especially food, were fair game when the occupants had left. The house adjoining the north side of Moses McClean's building was rented from the McCleans by a Mr. William Guinn. Guinn and his family fled town before the Confederate occupation. The McCleans did their best to watch over the empty house and were successful by taking bold measures. At some point during the morning of July 3rd, Robert McClean was sitting on his 2nd floor, rear balcony. From his vantage point in the shadows, he spotted a lone soldier trying to climb through a rear window in the Guinn's house. Realizing that from where the intruder stood he was practically invisible, Robert shouted out a stern command: "Get out of there, that is private property, you have no business there." Without hesitation the soldier turned and went away. Robert's siblings playfully teased him: "If he could have seen the boy who had called to him, maybe he would not have gone away as quickly as he did."[6]

In the Hollinger's neighborhood the Confederates had taken over several houses that had been abandoned. They helped themselves to whatever they wanted and there was nothing the Hollingers could do to stop them. They still put up a defiant front. One group of soldiers, feasting from the larder of a next door neighbor, called from the house to the Hollinger girls for butter to eat with biscuits they had baked. Liberty's younger sister Julia responded with brave defiance: "If you are hungry you can eat them as they are." This drew a laugh from the men. After the battle, when the refugees returned to their ransacked homes, some blamed the Hollingers for not keeping the Confederates out and protecting their valuables. The Hollingers were upset by this attitude. Liberty recalled: "We felt somewhat indignant, after our terrible experiences to have some of neighbors blame us, because we did not watch over their homes and protect their property. They ignored the ruin and destruction of our own property, which we had been powerless to prevent." These self-centered people were insensitive to the fact, "..that to save lives was the sole concern of those frightful days, property and material things faded into the background."[7]

Stores also fell prey to looting and ransacking when vacated by their proprietors. Next door to the Globe Inn was the grocery store owned by Joseph Gillespie. The anxiety created by the fear of the enemy and the possible shelling of the town proved too much for him and he locked his store and left. The Confederates broke the lock and "gutted" the store of its contents. What they did not want, they trampled under their feet. A liquor store a few houses away got the same treatment when the owner, Mr. Eaton, abandoned the premises. Unlike the grocery store, it is doubtful that any of Eaton's stock was left for the pleasures of mindless foot trampling. [8]

By mid day the weather was hot. The combination of over burdened privies, the decomposition of the bodies of men and horses still lying unburied in the town, thousands of unwashed bodies, and the decaying of amputated flesh deposited outside of the hospitals, were beginning to make the air in Gettysburg putrid. Nellie Aughinbaugh was a witness to the severed limbs that piled up to the window sills of her uncle's store, turned hospital, next door to her home. She recalled: "..they lay there in the sweltering sun of July." It was not until sometime after the Confederates left that, "..they came with horses and carts, shoveled the amputated parts up and hauled them away."[9] It was a scene repeated all over town, wherever there was a hospital. The exigencies of war did not allow for the timely tidying up of the battlefield.

A nonchalance began to set in with some of the population, particularly with the youth. Albertus McCreary described it: "We got used...to the fighting and curiosity got the better of us." This indifference to the sudden violence of battle and the seriousness of the enemy occupying the town nearly proved disastrous to young McCreary that morning. Following the cessation of the fighting on Culp's Hill there was a lull on the battlefield, disturbed only by the continued firing between skirmishers. Albertus and his brother decided the silence of the big guns meant it was generally safe and decided to go up on their roof and have a look around. Poking their upper bodies through the roof trap door, while standing on a ladder, provided them, "..with a good view." Houses south of them appeared, "..to be full of sharpshooters." They noticed a neighbor on his roof enjoying the same view they were. Then came a moment that was cause for their amusement. Albertus recalled: "He (the neighbor) was peeping around the chimney when a bullet struck just above his head and knocked off a piece of brick. He disappeared so quickly that we laughed." The boys' enjoyment was brought to an abrupt ending. Quickly following the disappearance of their neighbor, two bullets plowed into the shingles of the McCreary roof next to their perch. They immediately, "..followed the example of our neighbor." Doubtless this was no cause for their amusement.[10]

The roof top lesson on the seriousness and danger of war was soon forgotten. A short time later the impetuous Albertus was out on High Street by his side porch, wearing a discarded Union kepi. His impudence nearly cost him his freedom. Thinking nothing about the possible consequence of wearing an item of Federal uniform clothing, he stood watching a squad of Confederate infantry march up the street. As they came abreast of where he was, the detail was halted. An order dispatched two soldiers to his side and they seized him. Albertus was gripped with fear. Resisting his captors, he shouted for his father. The elder McCreary appeared at the door and inquired of the officer in charge as to what was the matter.

"He is in the army and must come with us," was the reply.

"Oh, no. He is only a school boy," laughed his father.

The Confederate officer saw no humor in the masquerade and insisted that Albertus was a prisoner of war. Only after neighbors, drawn to the street by the disturbance, confirmed David McCreary's story did the officer consent to let Albertus go.[11]

Elsewhere in the town, life had settled into a routine. People stayed in their houses unless it was absolutely necessary to go out into the street.[12] The care for the wounded in the makeshift hospitals and private homes went on without a break. Salome Myers now had four patients in her house and she was spending less time at the hospital in the Catholic Church in order to care for her wards at home.[13]

Agnes Barr and her sisters continued to work around the clock at the stove. The movement of the food from her kitchen to the church during daylight hours was hazardous. The presence of Confederate soldiers in the adjoining alley on the south side of the house drew a steady fire from Federal sharpshooters on Cemetery Hill. Bullets continually flew across the Barr's backyard and along Baltimore Street in the front. It was necessary for members of the household to get the all clear from the Confederates in the alley before venturing to the backyard well pump. Food bearers ran a dangerous gauntlet, usually down the rear alley, to the church, but no one was ever hit.[14]

At approximately 1 P.M. the lull on the battlefield ended with two shots fired in rapid succession by designated Confederate signal guns. A crescendo of artillery fire began immediately. It surpassed anything the townspeople had endured before. Everyone rushed to the safety of their cellars. The shells were once again screeching over Gettysburg. Sarah Broadhead, crowded into the Troxel cellar, was impressed with, "..the terrific sound of the strife, more terrible never greeted human ears." The bombardment lasted a long time and the people in the safety of the cellar turned their thoughts to those who were the targets for the deadly missiles. Sarah recorded the moment in her diary: "We knew that with every explosion...human beings were hurried through excruciating pain into another world and that many more were torn, mangled and lying in torment worse than death... The thought made me very sad." Almost as tormenting as the thoughts of the killed and wounded was the prospect of the outcome of this great assault: "We knew that the Confederates were putting forth all their might and it was a dreadful thought that they might succeed."[15]

The people in the Jacobs' cellar reacted to the noise of the bombardment and the shells passing overhead in a variety of ways. Several people eased their tension by making a game out of the artillery duel. Two young ladies who were refugees from the nearby countryside, amused themselves by identifying the origin of the cannon fire. As the cannons made their thunderous calls and responses they would exclaim: "Their side-Our side! Their side-Our side!" Whenever there was a pause in the Federal return fire they would anxiously cry out: "Oh, we've stopped." When the Federal gunners resumed, the ladies shouted with joy: "There it is again. Our side-Their side!" Henry Jacobs recalled the event in more somber terms: "It was such a duel as forced the sense of hearing...to grope amid the thundering chaos and to leave the mind almost dazed by concussions."[16]

At the David McCreary house the great cannonade was also remembered for its impact on the senses. In his memoirs, Albertus recalled: "The vibrations could be felt and the atmosphere was so full of smoke that we could taste the saltpeter." Jennie McCreary, who lived on Chambersburg Street, had recollections that paralleled those of Henry Jacobs. Describing the experience in a letter to her sister she wrote: "The cannonading began and such cannonading no one ever heard. Nothing can be compared to it. No one who never heard it can form any idea of how terrible it is." She felt the cannonade was the beginning of a decisive action: "All felt that the day must decide who should conquer."[17]

After an hour and a half the cannonade suddenly ceased and a lull on the battlefield followed. Dazed citizens emerged from their dungeons and wondered what it meant. A few recognized the lull to be a prelude to a decisive infantry attack, and hurried up to their garrets for a better view of the upcoming action. Michael Jacobs left his basement and grabbed his telescope on his way to the garret. He trained it on Seminary Ridge: "There, as though I was almost upon them I beheld Pickett's Division swinging into position." Watching the Confederates march across the intervening fields, Michael called to his son: "Quick! Come! Come! You can see now what in your life you will never see again."[18]

At the McCurdy house, young Charles and his dad hurried to their upper floor for the same purpose. They met with disappointment. The scene was over a mile away and "a dense volume of smoke hid everything from view." Albertus McCreary waved off the near miss he had experienced earlier that day and returned to his roof. He met with the same disappointment as the McCurdys, too much smoke to see anything. Soon the noise arising out of the fog shrouding the Union positions reached a crescendo and then ebbed. It was all over and a uneasy quiet settled over the town.[19]

The quiet did not apply to everyone. Agnes Barr ventured out of her house for the first time in two days and ran head-on into all the war she would ever care to know. Foodstuff for the hospital in the Presbyterian Church was running low. Agnes was determined to go across Baltimore street to solicit bread from the families living there. She popped out her front door and headed for Dr. John Runkel's house situated across the street and four doors south. She made the trip over without any difficulty. The Runkels finally opened up, blinking from the strong daylight. They had been down in their basement since Wednesday afternoon and had nothing in the way of bread to offer. Empty handed Agnes prepared for the trip back to her house. By crossing over to the Runkel's, she had alerted the Federal sharpshooters at the end of the street. Dr. Runkel urged her not to risk the danger and to stay with them until dark. Agnes recalled the moment and her decision: "They alarmed me as I did know how to get back, but I started." Putting her head down she made a dash for home with Confederates in the alley on both sides of the street laughing and cheering her on. It was a close call, but she made it: "As I got to my front door the bullets came down the street."[20]

As evening turned to dusk, Confederate troops returned from the field to the streets of town. William McClean and his wife felt uneasy . The Confederates were, "..sullen and gloomy," and were taking defensive measures such as building barricades to fight off a potential Federal assault. The possibility of fighting around their house was a "..depressing prospect." The McCleans invited a North Carolina officer to dinner and, "..solicited his protection of the house." He promised to do everything within his power, but his hosts still felt apprehensive. William recalled: "We laid ourselves down not knowing what to expect."[21]

Most of the Confederate soldiers obviously were in the same state of mind. They too did not know what to expect come tomorrow. At least one citizen, Belle King, seemed to sense their mood and used the uncertainty to play some mind games with her captors. After dark she brought some fresh made biscuits into Martha Scott's kitchen. There she encountered two young Confederates serving as door guards.

"Now eat some," she admonished them.

"We had a right good supper" was the reply.

"Well then put them in your knapsacks. You can eat them on your retreat."

"Oh, we are not going to retreat," the two responded.

"Why, yes. McClellan (popular, former commander of the Army of the Potomac) will be here before morning with a big army," Belle declared.

With worried glances the two boys put the biscuits into their knapsacks and silently returned to their post at the front door.[22]

Sometime after dark, a small group of Confederate soldiers knocked on the kitchen door at the Garlachs. A wary Catherine Garlach inquired as to who was there, and what was their purpose. The Confederates stated their business. They wanted permission to use the cabinet shop to make a coffin for one of their slain officers. Mrs. Garlach refused out of concern for the safety of her family. They would need light by which to work and she feared this would make the house a target for Union sharpshooters on Cemetery Hill. They were welcome to take what lumber they needed from the ample supply in the back yard. She suggested they carry it into town to Daniel Culp's shop next to the courthouse. There they would be out of danger from the sharpshooters. They followed her advice and proceeded to Culp's house with the lumber in tow. The cabinetmaker agreed to let them use his shop to build the coffin. The order to retreat interrupted the work, and the Confederates left it behind, unfinished and unused. Anna Garlach believed the coffin was finished the next day and was used to bury the body of Jennie Wade in the garden behind her sister's house.[23]

Others in town noticed a distinct change in the attitude of the Confederates. Sarah Broadhead noted in her diary: "Some think the Rebels have been defeated as there has been no boasting..and they look uneasy and by no means exultant." Even Catherine Foster, who heretofore had found the Confederates very communicative, remarked on the change in attitude: " Our Rebels became reticent. They gave us no more information."[24]

Nerves were quite naturally strained at this point of the ordeal. Confederates and captive Union surgeons had been living side by side in the Globe Inn with very little difference in their respective status of freedom. Until the climactic events of July 3rd the foes got along remarkably well. The Confederate setback that day brought about a change in the status quo. That evening, in the hotel barroom, two Confederate officers and two Union surgeons were sharing conversation and refreshments when a bitter quarrel broke out. John Will was there in the company of Miss Tillie Gillespie, a neighbor who had come in during the afternoon's cannonade to seek safer surroundings. According to John, the quarrel escalated to the point of a fight. Out of respect for Miss Gillespie, John interceded to stop blows from being struck and possible bloodshed. The parties regained some composure and agreed, "..to settle the matter somewhere else in the near future."[25]

There was another change in Confederate behavior that night. They undertook another search of many residences looking for hidden Federal soldiers cut off in Wednesday's retreat. Citizens caught harboring fugitives could look forward to a harsh penalty, perhaps incarceration in a southern prison. It has never been established what precipitated a renewal of this search activity which had been largely discontinued since Wednesday. Reasonable speculation can be made that the Confederates were tipped off by a local southern sympathizer(s) to the fact that a number of the enemy were still at large in the town. John Will was emphatic on the point that such people were numerous in the, "border counties," and that he knew, "..Adams County had its share."[26]

1st block of Baltimore St. Oct. 1863, Professor Martin Stover's 3 story house is on far right. (ACHS)

For whatever cause the Confederates conducted a number of raids that night after the town had settled down to sleep. The Moses McClean household was jolted awake by the noise of a Confederate detail, "..forcing open the cellar door on the front pavement." There had been no knock at the door to request admittance. This was a sudden, unannounced invasion of private property by force, which was unprecedented in the Confederate behavior towards the civilians in Gettysburg. Elizabeth McClean recalled: "My father went down and they said they were looking for Yankee soldiers. They found none...only some cartridges that had been left there by the soldiers (captured there following Wednesday's retreat)."[27]

The party then moved two houses to the north and entered the basement of Professor Martin Stoever's house. Here they found three unlucky soldiers who had been concealed and sustained by the Stoevers since Wednesday afternoon. The captives were marched off. A short while later the Confederates returned with orders to arrest the Professor. Stoever refused to open the door and pleaded his case from a second story window. He felt concern for the safety of the women in the house during the night, and he promised to report himself to the Provost Marshal's office the first thing in the morning. This arrangement was finally agreed upon and the Stoever family joined the rest of Gettysburg in a restless sleep.[28]

JULY 4TH: "..resurrected from an untold ordeal"

The beginning of the Confederate withdrawal from the town was first noticed by some light sleepers during the early hours of the morning. Mary McAllister, dozing in a chair at her front window, was awakened by wagons moving out Chambersburg Street. Quickly comprehending the meaning of the traffic she awakened Martha with the declaration: "I believe the Confederates are retreating." Martha was awake in an instant, but was not as certain as Mary about the Confederate's intentions: "Oh, if it is only true, for I am hardly able to go it."

A short time later Mary got confirmation of her hunch: "..a man came running down the street and awakened the guards at her front door and said, Get up! Get Up! We are retreating." As the guards were gathering their possessions (including Belle King's biscuits) in preparation to join the exodus, Mary suppressed a unusual emotion in light of all that she had endured: "I wanted to say goodby, but it would have sounded like mockery."[1] Now that her ordeal was lifting, was she feeling a bond born out of gratitude toward her captors for their humane conduct?

Robert McClean, a light sleeper like Mary McAllister, was awakened at 2 A.M. by a horseman on the street in front of his house directing soldiers to, "..go down to the railroad and turn left." Agnes Barr heard rumors at her house and she could not go back to sleep. In fact, Agnes claimed that she was the first to notify the Federal troops that the Rebels were gone: "We took a flag of truce and carried the first news to the Federal army out at Cemetery Hill."[2]

There is some evidence that may confirm Agnes' claim. Henry Monath, a member of Co.I, 74th PA., was part of the Federal skirmish detail stationed in the Wagon Hotel at the junction of Baltimore Street and the Emmitsburg Road. Monath recalled that at the first signs of dawn sentinels called him and his companions out into the road. From there, "..we could see the citizens on the street waving their handkerchiefs for us to come." Monath recalled that he and about 20 others, "..decided we would move into the city." Checking houses as they cautiously proceeded up Baltimore Street, they found numerous Rebel soldiers sleeping who they quietly took as prisoners. By the time they reached the square they had nearly a hundred captives in tow. Confirming that the Confederates had vacated the town, Monath and his companions returned with their prisoners to the Wagon Hotel. Monath claimed that following his report to his commanding officer on the status in Gettysburg: "..the army commenced to come straggling into the city."[3]

Most of the town's residents slept through the Confederate withdrawal and were awakened by the commotion surrounding the entry of the Federal troops. The discovery that their nightmare had ended left everyone with common feelings of joy and relief. Even the drenching showers could not dampen the people's elation. Jennie McCreary described the mood of the town that morning: "How happy everyone felt. None but smiling faces were to be seen..."[4]

Each remembered their moment of liberation in slightly different ways, but the pure elation of the event was present in all their memoirs. Daniel Skelly recalled the Federal entry into town as a parade: "It was a noisy demonstration. The boys in blue marching down the street (Baltimore), fife and drum corps playing, the glorious Stars and Stripes fluttering at the head of the lines." The discovery of the Confederate withdrawal reminded Catherine Foster of another time when freedom was celebrated: "Oh..the Glorious Fourth of July. The voices of the citizens were again heard greeting each other from their windows, as if they had been resurrected from an untold ordeal..." Sarah Broadhead too was filled with joy when she looked up Chambersburg Street and saw: "..our men in the public square, and it was a joyous sight, for I knew we were now safe." At the Scott's house, the reaction was much the same as Sarah's. Mary McAllister remembered it vividly: "..the first thing we knew a Union band began to play and I think I never knew anything sweeter, and I never felt so glad in my life."[5]

Alice Powers was moved in a different way, perhaps because the liberation of the town did not remove the awful reality of the suffering of the helpless wounded. She described her reaction to the news: "Dr. James Fulton came into the room where we were attending the wounded and told us to come out and sing the 'Star Bangled Banner' for the Rebels had gone. Sure enough when we went to the door, the last gray coat was seen going out the end of the street. With thankful hearts, yet too sad to sing, we hurried back to the rest with the glad news."[6]

The vast majority of the people probably bowed their heads for a few minutes and inwardly rejoiced while offering prayers of thanks. At least one citizen needed to seek confirmation of the fact before allowing himself to believe it was really true. John Will was awakened by the commotion and stepped out onto the balcony to see the cause of the ruckus. In the first rays of light he saw, "..a company of Union troops on the Diamond." Not certain what this could mean he went back inside and checked the rooms used by the Confederates: "..and found them gone." He then believed that it was over.[7]

Others were seized by a compulsion to engage in some sort of immediate activity to insure that the menace of the past three days was over and gone. Dr. Charles Horner's wife, Caroline, was driven to remove all physical reminders of the battle that touched her house. When Mary McAllister came downstairs shortly after daybreak to look out her door at the Federal troops in the square, she encountered Mrs. Horner on her hands and knees, "..scrubbing the mud and blood," from her front pavement.[8]

Some of the men took a more direct approach. Robert McLean recalled: "Citizens assisted in hunting up Confederate stragglers." It had the potential for being risky business. On the south end of town on Baltimore St., James Pierce came out of his front door in his stocking feet, picked up a discarded rifle from the pavement, and began corralling tardy Confederates still lingering in the backyards adjoining his property. He quickly garnered three and turned them over to nearby Union soldiers. Returning to the rear alley he encountered another who was still armed. At Pierce's command to halt, the Rebel confronted him for a long minute before deciding to give way; perhaps influenced by Pierce's threat to fire. After this episode Pierce finally checked his weapon, only to discover that it was not loaded. At the McClean household, Robert and his younger brother went Rebel hunting, but without being armed. Fortunately for them there was no reason to fear the consequences: "Colin and myself found one on our stable loft, fast asleep."[9]

It was a welcome relief for the fugitive soldiers who had eluded capture throughout the Confederate occupation. As blue columns moved down the streets into the town they began to emerge from their hiding places. On E. High Street a Union soldier came down from the public school belfry where he had hidden since the time of the retreat. He had sustained himself for two and a half days on nothing more than a few pieces of hard tack and a canteen of water. At Catherine Foster's, Cpl. Wilcox came out from, "..his cave under the kitchen," and headed off to find his regiment. The five soldiers hiding at the Pierce house could finally come outside as their own troops marched down Baltimore Street. It was the same a few doors farther south at the Garlach house. As soon as it was light, Catherine Garlach hurried outside to check on General Schimmelfennig. He had not waited for her to tell him it was all clear. As Catherine came out the kitchen door she spied him walking, "..stiff and cramped like..," across her neighbor's yard toward the Federal lines. The first troops he encountered: "..proved to be his own men. They thought he had been killed and when they saw him, they went wild with delight."[10]

It was also a moment for great joy and relief in Professor Stoever's household. By virtue of the Confederate withdrawal from town, the Professor was released from his commitment to surrender himself. This unquestionably saved him from a stay in a Confederate prison.

The rejoicing was tempered for soldier and civilian alike, as movement across the east-west avenues brought rifle fire into town from the direction of Seminary Ridge. Lee had not begun a retreat from the area. Instead he had consolidated his lines into a defensive position along Seminary Ridge and awaited an attack from his adversary. His picket line was posted at the western edge of town behind a small stream known as Stevens Run. From here his sharpshooters were firing on any target showing itself along Chambersburg, High and Middle streets. As bullets flew, they quickly reminded everyone that neither the fighting nor the danger were over. Henry Jacobs was horrified to witness a Union horseman shot through the arm as he attempted to cross the intersection beside his house. Henry tried to rationalize what had just taken place: "It was the Confederates way of covering their retreat, and no doubt it was war, but it looked like murder to an eyewitness." His younger sister Julia was equally horrified and decided then and there to do something to neutralize the deadly ambush. She stood at the front door of the Jacobs house and called a warning to anyone blindly approaching the corner along S. Washington Street: "Look Out! Pickets below! They'll fire on you!" She became a living warning flag. The Confederates caught on and turned their rifles on the door entrance in an attempt to silence her. Julia merely backed deeper into the doorway and continued to call her warning until Federal infantry came up and threw a barricade across the street. From behind the protective wall, they took on the Rebel marksmen. Julia's dangerous and heroic mission was completed.[11]

Just before Julia began warning the unsuspecting of the danger, a young girl almost fell prey to a sharpshooter's bullet at this intersection (S. Washington and Middle Streets). Twelve year old Mary Warren was walking on the north pavement along Middle Street, returning to her home at the west end of town. She had been sent to her grandfather's house on Baltimore Street the morning before. Her parents had felt she would be safer there than in their own home. As soon as the Federal troops passed by her grandfather's, "..hurrahing for the Fourth of July..," Mary started for home. As she approached the intersection at S. Washington Street: "I heard something whistle past my ear." Then a familiar voice shouted, "Mary!" It was her father who was standing across the street along the east side of the Michael Jacobs house. He dashed across Washington Street and pulled her into the safety of Elizabeth Minnigh's side yard, next to where Mary stood anchored in fear. The Warren house was only a block and a half from the Confederate skirmish line and totally inaccessible. The Minnighs took Mary in until the Confederate skirmishers withdrew and it was safe to walk the streets.[12]

It was a trying morning for both daughter and father. Hiram Warren was just returning from uptown where he had been held by Federal troops for being a Confederate straggler. He was wearing a gray suit. Only the testimony of fellow townspeople, as to the fact that he was indeed a civilian citizen, secured his release. He was on route home to change his clothes when he encountered Mary. Unable to reach his home because of the Confederate rifle fire, he underwent the same humiliating experience several more times during the day. "Halt or be shot," was the command. Then followed the routine of being dragged before the Provost Marshal to establish his civilian status. For Warren, the ordeal fostered upon the citizens by the occupation of their town was not over even though the Confederates had evacuated. Cut off from his home as he was, his personal freedom remained indirectly under Confederate control for most of the day.[13]

The sharpshooting into town by the Confederates disrupted other families. Gates Fahnestock and other members of his family went outside on the pavement along the side of their house to sweep the debris left by the Confederates camping there for the past two days. They had barely begun the task, when, "..a bullet grazed the side of the house above our heads," driving them all back inside: "We kept off that pavement for the remainder of the day."[14]

At Professor Stoever's house the family was just finishing breakfast when a knock came at the front door. It was a Federal officer who politely, but firmly, demanded the use of his 3rd floor for sharpshooters, since the building was one of the tallest in town. It was a demand that could not be refused. The Stoever's concluded: "It would not be safe for the family to remain." Mrs. Stoever and the children packed some clothes and left town for several days. It seems ironic that, as the battle was coming to a conclusion, a family was forced to evacuate the town after having already endured the hardships of the Confederate occupation.[15]

Two doors away, the Moses McClean family decided to follow suit, but they did not evacuate the town. According to Robert: "Uncle Stoever's house was occupied by sharpshooters. Fearing the enemy might shell the houses occupied by sharpshooters we picked up..and went to brother William's (on E. Middle Street) for the day."[16]

The exchange of rifle fire in the town on July 4th did not precipitate a general evacuation by the population. People were accustomed to the danger and simply endured it by staying out of the line of fire. All were not successful. A few civilians, as well as soldiers, suffered wounds at the hands of Rebel marksmen. Jacob Gilbert was on the pavement outside Harvey Wattle's house on W. Middle Street when a bullet found his left arm, "..making a flesh wound." Gilbert used the back alleys to get himself to Dr. Horner's on Chambersburg Street where the wound was dressed.[17]

Mary McAllister crossed Chambersburg St. to visit Sarah Jane Weikert, two doors west of the church. As she approached the house Amos Whetstone, a Seminary student and boarder, called out from the back porch to warn her of the danger: "Take care or you will be shot." In his next breath, Whetstone exclaimed: "Oh, I believe I am shot!" A quick examination revealed that he had received a bullet "through the fleshy part of his leg." The July 7th issue of THE ADAMS SENTINEL, named two other citizens (in addition to Gilbert, Whetstone and John Burns) as wounded, probably on July 4th. None of the wounds were serious.[18] There was trauma for at least one citizen that was not caused by the sniper fire. The Union soldiers had erected a barricade across the upper end of Chambersburg Street to protect against incoming bullets from the Confederate marksmen to the west. Some broken down horses had gotten free from somewhere and were aimlessly wandering about the streets and the square. A few of these animals strayed into Chambersburg Street and started west along the pavement. When they encountered the barrier of the breastworks they turned into an open front door and passed along the hall through the house onto the wooden back porch. They panicked at this point and began to lose their footing on the porch deck made slippery by the rain. As horses began to sprawl and fall into the yard, the poor woman occupying the house threw up her hands in exasperation: "Oh Lord, what will come next?"[19]

Sometime during the morning a rumor that the Rebels were going to shell the town spread through Gettysburg. In an instant the familiar panic and anxiety returned. People scurried to their cellars. Others made hurried plans to flee the town. Fortunately it did not happen and the panic subsided.[20] The episode did serve to jolt the general population out of their euphoria and bring them back into reality. Despite the withdrawal by the Confederates, the state of affairs in the town was still pretty grim. The big problems were the shortage of food, and the overwhelming number of wounded requiring care and attention.

The Federal soldiers merely replaced the Confederates in terms of demand on the town's food supply. The army's supply system had not kept up with the rapid marches of the troops concentrating on Gettysburg. To make matters worse the railroad line into Gettysburg was damaged for some miles to the east and supplies could not be brought in by that means. The nearest supply depot was twenty miles away in Westminster, Maryland and food and medicine had to hauled in by wagon. In 48 hours the railroad would be repaired and relief would start to arrive in huge quantities. In the meantime, soldiers were hungry and begged for food where they could get it. Grateful civilians responded to the best of their means, but there just was not enough to feed everyone.[21]

There was the battle debris. Bodies of men and horses left from Wednesday's fighting still lay about the town. By Saturday their decomposition had advanced to the point of being offensive. The bodies of the men were gathered up and buried that day, but the horses remained untouched.[22] Barricades constructed across the streets and alleys made free movement difficult. On top of this came a violent thunderstorm, that poured torrential rains onto the town and surrounding countryside through most of the night. Under cover of the rain and darkness Lee pulled in his skirmishers and began his retreat toward the Potomac River and Virginia.

The entry for the day in Sarah Broadhead's diary summed up Saturday, July 4th, for all citizens in Gettysburg: "It has been a dreadfully long day..but the day is ended and all is quiet, and for the first time for a week I shall go to bed feeling safe."[23]

July 5th - August 1st:
"..the people of Gettysburg assisted in everyway"

Dawn on Sunday morning was rainy and dreary, but memorable for the absence of fighting. The last of the Confederate columns were preparing to get underway. This day would prove to be a breather before the next invasion of Gettysburg would begin. The invasion of thousands from around the country to help with the wounded, to seek loved ones living and dead, and to see the battlefield. Together they would take Gettysburg by storm and overwhelm the hospitality of an emotionally and physically exhausted population.

Gettysburg awoke to an intensifying putrid atmosphere that would not completely disappear until the frosts of fall. The stench of rotting flesh from the surrounding countryside, mixed with the odor rising from improperly managed human excretions left by the soldiers in town, created an air that was barely breathable. According to Albertus McCreary, beginning this day and for weeks to follow: "the stench was so bad...that everyone went around with a bottle of pennyroyal or peppermint oil." Nellie Aughinbaugh recalled: "We could not open our windows for weeks because of the terrible stench."[1]

The burial of the battle dead had begun the day before, but many had already lain untouched for four days in the July heat by the time they were covered. The grave digging was done by soldiers in an expedited fashion. There was still a dangerous enemy to be pursued and little time for battlefield policing. The graves were shallow and many were uncovered by the heavy rains. The dead horses left on the field were estimated to be between three and five thousand. After the soldiers were buried these animals were dragged into piles and burned; an extremely slow and odorous process.

This attracted insects by the millions, especially flies. In the humid, hot days of July, hordes of these pests fed on the decaying flesh found in the field hospitals and partially covered graves, and invaded the town carrying fever inducing germs. The town fought the threat of disease by daily spreading chloride of lime on the streets to disinfect the mud, manure and puddles that accumulated there. The peculiar smell of the disinfectant mingled with the other noxious odors to add to the unpleasantness of the atmosphere. At night it became necessary to sleep with the windows shut, keeping out the odor, but keeping in the heat of the day. William McClean remembered: "When you opened the windows for the morning air, you would be assailed by the foul odors. We citizens became gradually acclimated to it, but some visitors became ill, left for home and some died."[2]

Besides the assault of the foul odor on their senses, the townspeople faced an ever growing food crisis. The Aughinbaugh's, who left the day before when they heard the town would be shelled, returned to find, "..their fine garden full of vegetables.." decimated. Nellie commented: "All we found was about a quart of beans. They had to suffice for a family of eight..."[3]

Relief was on the way. The U.S. Sanitary Commission, the Christian Commission and other relief organizations were marshaling vast quantities of foodstuff and medical supplies for the wounded and moving on Gettysburg. The vanguard of this effort would arrive by wagon from Westminster, Md. before dark on the 5th. By July 7th the railroad would be able to come as far as the burned out bridge at Rock Creek, bringing more supplies and people. Meanwhile civilians and soldiers alike would have to do the best they could.

During the day of the 5th, the bond of adversity that had held the citizens of Gettysburg in such tight unity over the past ten days began to loosen. Some ugly incidents of citizen turning on citizen occurred. Strong partisan politics had long been the norm in Adams County and in Gettysburg. More recently the Republicans had formed a Union League chapter in the area to tout patriotic feelings in support of the conduct of the war. By inference or outright proclamation, zealots in this group labeled Democrats as anti-patriotic. Now that the immediate threat from the Confederates had passed, the old animosities between town Republicans and Democrats began to re-emerge.

The first sign was the sudden arrest by the army provost guard of Charles and John Will, proprietors of the Globe Inn and staunch Democrats. A citizen(s) had reported them to the authorities for "harboring Confederates." The Wills', in the company of attorney J.Cassat Neely, argued that they had treated the Confederates as paying guests, and had showed no favor or offered no aid. Indeed, they demonstrated that they had suffered the loss of stolen whiskey at the hands of their guests. They also claimed, "the charge was brought against us through political enmity." The Provost Marshal heard their case and agreed with them: "I am convinced there is political feeling between you people." The charges were dropped.[4]

Right on the heels of this case came charges against Henry Stahle, editor of THE COMPILER. These charges were also patently false, but they stuck. His alleged accuser was David McConaughy, a local attorney, and a very influential and outspoken Republican. Stahle's act of going to the courthouse and procuring a Confederate surgeon to come to his home and treat the leg of Col. William W. Dudley on July 1st, was interpreted by his accuser as aiding the enemy in apprehending a Union officer attempting to avoid capture. He was arrested on those charges. Despite eyewitness testimony, including that of Col. Dudley, exonerating Stahle of any such intent, he was held and incarcerated in Ft. McHenry in Baltimore. There, higher authorities would have nothing to do with such a sham. After a week he was released and returned to Gettysburg.[5]

First block of Chambersburg St. (south side), Oct, 1863. McCurdy house 2nd from the right. (GRB)

The same motivation may have been behind the complaints, "..by certain citizens," against the care Confederate Major General Isaac Trimble received at the home of Robert McCurdy. The General had lost a leg to a wound received while leading a division in the grand and unsuccessful assault on the Union center. Following the surgery at the College hospital, he was brought to the McCurdy household by Federal soldiers for care, until he was recovered sufficiently to be transported to a prisoner of war camp. McCurdy, a moderate Democrat, agreed to take in the General. The whole time he was there, Trimble was considered a prisoner of war. The complaints were filed with the Federal military authorities two weeks after he was placed with the McCurdys. As a result, he was removed to a hospital and denied any special considerations. No action was taken against his former host, which may have been a disappointment to the unnamed complainants.[6]

Altercations involving citizens were not limited to inter- political party shenanigans. During the evening of the 5th, poor Mary Wade, the mother of Jennie, was back in her home on Breckenridge St. after burying her daughter the day before.

She was visited by a Rev. Walter Alexander of the Christian Commission who undoubtedly heard of her tragedy and came by to pay his respects and to offer sympathies. Also in the house was a Maj. Michael Burns of the 73rd NY Infantry. Burns was heavily intoxicated and for some unknown reason drew his sword and assaulted Reverend Alexander, seriously wounding him in the head. The stunned and hurt Reverend was led away for medical help, and the dangerous Maj. Burns was arrested. It is ironic that no such violent acts against citizens were reported during the Confederate occupation of Gettysburg.[7]

In stark contrast to the event at Mary Wade's, was the pleasant surprise that took place at Mary McAllister's house. The last of the wounded had just been transported across the street to the church. Mary and Martha were busily trying to restore some semblance of order to the house, when Mary was summoned to the front door. Two men, one of them David Wills, were on horseback at the pavement. The stranger opened the conversation.

"Miss Mary, don't you know me?"

"No! You look a little like Col. Morrow, but the Rebels took him."

"Why God bless you! I am Col. Morrow, safe and sound, and I called for my diary."

Then everything came back to Mary and she recalled taking the book and shoving it into her dress as the Confederates were entering her kitchen door on the afternoon of July 1st. The colonel went on to explain how he made good his escape from the College hospital posing as a surgeon. He found refuge at David Will's house for the duration of the Confederate occupation. Now he was recovered sufficiently to rejoin his unit. He had returned to the Scott's in the company of David Wills to reclaim his diary. Mary fetched it from inside the house and brought along General Archer's sword as well. Rearmed, Morrow bid his farewell and hastened off to overtake his comrades.[8]

On Monday, July 6th, the people of Gettysburg had recovered sufficiently from their own ordeal to turn their full attention to the wounded, whose numbers still overwhelmed the facilities and surgeons available to treat them. The horrors continued in the courthouse hospital and daily Fannie Buehler sent over all the food she could spare. She recalled: "The sights and sounds at the courthouse for a week following the battle are too horrible to describe. Limbs were amputated amid the cries and groans of suffering humanity...I stopped my ears that I might not hear the groans of those poor unfortunate men..Loads of arms and legs..were carted outside of town and buried." Regimental bands, left behind to shore up morale of the injured, appeared each day outside the courthouse and played patriotic songs.[9]

The William McLean's scraped together all the food they could find, "biscuits and gruel," and basket in hand headed out the Chambersburg Pike to the McPherson farm. The wounded there were reported to be suffering from untended wounds and little or no food. At the Myers house the number of convalescents from the Catholic Church hospital had grown to fourteen. Salome busied herself nearly around the clock tending the suffering, some of whom did not recover. On the 6th she lost Sgt. Alexander Stewart, who if he had lived would have been her future brother-in-law. Salome did not have a bed in which to sleep until the wounded were moved to Camp Letterman in late July. At the Solomon Powers house, just a few doors from the Myers', the scene was the same. The Powers girls, along with their refugee guests, Catherine and Lizzie Sweney, were caring for some, "..fifteen or sixteen..", invalid wounded. They demonstrated a real talent for nursing skills. It was reported that soldiers' wounds were dressed and bandaged as skillfully as would have been done, "..by the most expert nurse..."[10]

Lutheran Seminary as seen from the Chambersburg Pike, ca 1870. (GNMP)

Sarah Broadhead along with others went as a group to the Seminary building with the small amount of food they could gather. The evidence of the brutal fighting strewn across the ground they walked over, tested their resolve: "What horrible sights present themselves on every side...Shall we enter the building or return home? Can we endure the spectacle of hundreds of men wounded in every conceivable manner...? What can we do?" With stiff upper lips they forged ahead and distributed their meager offering of food. The plight of the men inside was beyond their imagination and literally overwhelmed Sarah: "I turned away and cried." Her stay the first time was brief, but possessing true grit, she returned the next day with food and bravely undertook to assist with the care of the wounded. It was not easy: "I procured a basin and water and went into a room where there were seven or eight..I asked for his wound and he pointed toward his leg. Such a horrible sight I have never seen and I hope never to see again. His leg was all covered with worms. We fixed the man as comfortably as we could..." Sarah went home that night, "..very much fatigued and worn out..," to record her experience in her diary. She wrote for all the civilian women of Gettysburg who fought back their fears, and without training of any sort, pitched in to aid and comfort the helpless wounded: "..having done what I never expected to do or thought I could. I am becoming more used to the sights of misery." She would go back the following days until the number of out-of-town volunteers, coming from around the nation, was sufficient to provide some relief for the Gettysburg women.[11]

July 6th was also the day by which most of the citizens who had fled the town to escape the fighting had returned. Catherine Ziegler and her family returned that day to their home in the Lutheran Seminary via the Emmitsburg road. Catherine recorded the scene that met their eyes as they neared town: "Pen can not describe the awful sights that met our gaze... Imagine if you can the stench of one dead animal lying in the hot July sun for days. Here they were by the hundreds." When they reached their destination they did not find the home they had left: "It was a ghastly sight to see, some of the men lying in pools of blood on the bare floors where they had been placed on July 1st, many having received no care whatever." The Zieglers tidied up their living quarters on the 1st floor and then turned to the task of caring for the wounded.[12]

Elizabeth Thorn and her family returned to their home in the Evergreen Cemetery gatehouse on July 7th. The destruction to the living quarters, from their use as a hospital, prohibited re-occupancy, and the Thorns moved into a tent in the rear yard. There was no time to clean up. Cemetery president David McConaughy ordered Elizabeth to lay out a number of new graves to re-bury Union soldiers. In the next three weeks Elizabeth and her father "dug 105 graves," working in the July heat and breathing air so fouled by the smell of rotting horses, "..that for days I could hardly eat." Elizabeth persevered this entire ordeal while being six months pregnant with her fourth child. Daughter Rosie Meade Thorn was born in October.[13]

Charles Tyson and his wife returned to their home from Littlestown on July 5th. They were greeted with a scene, that fortunately for them, was not typical for people who had elected to abandon their houses and flee the town. Tyson was nearly ecstatic at what he found: "I should feel very good upon entering my house to find nothing wantonly destroyed." Beyond liberating all the foodstuff, the Confederates had been merciful to the Tysons in comparison to their next door neighbor, William Boyer. That was the family whose house Sarah Broadhead had watched the Confederates loot on the night of July 1st. The scene that was usually encountered was experienced by a neighbor of Liberty Hollinger, who upon returning: "..found their once orderly house in confusion, bedroom bureaus ransacked, contents scattered over the house."[14]

Not every surprise for a family was a downer. The McCrearys were the happy benefactors of a most unusual occurrence. Forty six years after the event, Albertus McCreary retold the story: "We had an old cow that had been in the family for years, and on the morning of the 1st we put her in the pasture as usual near the edge of town. We saw nothing of her for the three days of fighting. The general opinion was that we had lost her. Father, brother and I went to look for her. We found many cow skins and heads and came to the conclusion that our cow had been butchered. A week or so after the battle, we heard a familiar bellow out in the street. There stood our dear cow."[15]

July 7th brought a lot of activity into the town. At least one sign of normalcy returned. The newspapers resumed publishing and for the first time in over a week were back on the streets. THE ADAMS SENTINEL for that day even attempted a little tongue-in-cheek humor. One of its' headlines ran: "OUR APOLOGY: We need scarce apologize to our readers for not making our usual visit to their homes last week. Only those with indifference to surroundings...can find fault. These we apprehend will be few."

The last remaining army divisions vacated the town and surrounding camps, and headed south and west to follow the Confederates in their retreat toward the Potomac River. They left behind 21,000 Union and Confederate wounded, and a skeleton force of surgeons, orderlies and provost guard.

A new army quickly took their place. The relief organizations, now arriving by rail, descended on the town in waves. Each arriving train brought a cadre of volunteers as well as food and medical provisions. It was a mixed blessing for the citizens of Gettysburg. The relief, particularly food, was desperately needed. The influx of outsiders arriving along with the food would overflow both the public and private capacity for accommodations. Once more the citizens of Gettysburg would extend themselves to meet the need.

The U.S. Sanitary Commission moved their headquarters and main supply distribution point into the center of town, taking over the Fahnestock Brothers store on the corner of Baltimore and Middle Streets. The Christian Commission followed suit, establishing their distribution headquarters at the north end of the block in the rooms of J.L. Schick's store, which occupied a portion of Professor

Fahnestock Brothers Store, July 9, 1863 (GNMP) serving as U.S. Sanitary Comm. warehouse.

Stoever's building. The majority of relief activity for the wounded in the various army hospitals, in and around the town, was coordinated from these two distribution points. The positive effect of their aid would be noticeable almost immediately, as care and living conditions for the wounded improved dramatically.

The citizens in Gettysburg directly benefitted from the presence of these organizations. Christian Commission volunteers began to spell many of them in the hospitals, giving exhausted Gettysburg women their first break since July 1st. Christian Commission field kitchens relieved Catherine Barr of her week long struggle to keep food prepared and available for the wounded in the Presbyterian Church, although the army surgeons there continued to board at her house.[16]

The Sanitary Commission provided a source of food to support the needs of the wounded under care of both the army and civilians alike. The supplies to the army field hospitals were provided gratis. There may have been double standards for the civilians whose homes were serving as hospitals. Fannie Buehler related a unusual story in her memoirs that suggests that such was the case: "For some days fresh meat was not to be had, but those who had wounded could order from the Sanitary Commission and get as much as they needed, by paying for it."[17]

On the other hand, Albertus McCreary's recollection of the Sanitary Commission's generosity seems to contradict the inference derived from Fannie's testimony: "All our beds were occupied (with wounded) and we boys slept on the floor and ate at the Sanitary Commission for weeks. The provisions we had in the house were soon consumed and if it had not been for the Commission we would have starved. We cooked Sanitary Commission food for our patients."[18] What is not debatable is the fact that the presence of the Commissions, their supplies and their many volunteers, relieved the local citizens from much of the burden that otherwise would have overwhelmed and crushed them.

The volunteers coming with the Commissions had to be housed and Gettysburg citizens took them into their homes. Professor Stoever put up two Christian Committee ladies in addition to the twelve wounded "guests" convalescing in his parlor and dining room.[19] Others did the same. Dr. Robert Horner took in a Miss Elizabeth Farnham, who turned his house into a mini depot by directing people back home to ship relief goods for the 2nd Corps hospital to her care at the Horner residence.[20] Civilian, volunteer doctors began to arrive in great numbers to augment the meager number of military surgeons left behind by the departed army. Many of these were housed in private homes in Gettysburg. Others stayed out at the field hospitals.[21]

The earliest relief for Gettysburg women serving in the town's hospitals arrived in the persons of the nuns from the Order of the Sister's of Charity in nearby Emmitsburg, Maryland. On the afternoon of July 5th a vanguard of 16 sisters established quarters in the McClellan House. Early the next morning they dispersed themselves among 5 hospitals, including the Courthouse and the Seminary, functioning as both nurse and doctor. They were followed by dozens more from their Order throughout the week.[22]

Another group of volunteer women known as the 'The Patriot Daughters of Lancaster' arrived on Friday the 10th. These ladies took on the responsibility for caring for the wounded housed in the Christ Lutheran Church on Chambersburg Street. There they quickly brought order from chaos by assuming all aspects of personal succor to the convalescing soldiers. After nearly a month they went home only to return within a week in response to the pleas of patients and surgeons alike. [23]

The influx of people continued daily. By July 8th relatives began to show up in numbers to search the hospitals for wounded loved ones, or worse yet to exhume a fresh grave. These anxious souls arrived at Gettysburg to find the hotels overflowing. John Will remembered: "We had no place for men. They occupied the carpets and floors of the parlor, even the loft in the stable. Women occupied all of our rooms."[24]

The overflow was taken into private homes. Gates Fahnestock's family hosted an entire delegation from Ohio, including "..Gov. Todd and Bishop McDaniel, a brother of a captain taken prisoner (at the house) on the 1st day." At Elizabeth

Mclean's household: "Our beds and tables were filled for weeks afterwards; we kept open house for relatives and friends and some others whom we never saw before and never saw again." The Hollingers found themselves having the identical experience with people, complete strangers, who were driven to desperate measures to find lodging. The Hollingers, like most other citizens in town obliged, but "..were amused and saddened by some visitors who claimed acquaintance in order to have a place to stay."[25]

The sharing of their homes and tables by the citizens was gratis, but there were those in town who found ways to make profit out of the circumstances. An impromptu hack industry evolved for the few who still had a horse and wagon. Leander Warren was one of the fortunate: "Every barn south and east (of town) was a hospital. People wanted someone to take them, so I made good use of our team." Often the return trip brought along a body wrapped in a muddy army blanket. [26]

The next stop was to another new industry born of necessity and circumstance, the embalming parlor. According to John Will, two embalmers arrived shortly after the battle ended and set up shop. One was located, "..in the room on York Street, next to Judge Wills' building and the other in the brick school house on the Mummasburg Road." Not surprisingly the establishment of a body processing industry had a positive ripple effect on the tavern business: "A number of our citizens made a quite a good thing out of this gruesome business, taking up bodies and assisting in preparing them for shipment home. Men engaged in this work bought whiskey in great quantities." Business remained brisk until the heat of the summer became so severe that the Provost Marshal halted the exhuming of graves on the field and at the hospitals until the cool of October. Then the vast majority were re-interred in the newly created Soldiers National Cemetery.[27]

A horse and wagon was not the only means for cashing in on opportunity. The battle field was literally covered with discarded tools of war. The initial wave of visitors contained a number of curiosity seekers who were eager to pick up a souvenir of the great battle. The abandoned war material was government property and strict rules against civilians removing it were quickly and rigorously enforced. People caught in the act of taking up or in possession of arms or accouterments were summarily arrested. Their penalty was several days of assisting in the battlefield cleanup; usually with the details disposing of the several thousand dead horses still rotting on the field. The army provost troops, assisted by these reluctant "volunteers," collected nearly twenty thousand rifles and almost as many sets of accouterments.

The vast amounts of lead bullets and unexploded shells lying on the ground were another matter. They were recyclable but not immediately useful to army ordnance personnel. The young boys in town quickly learned that agents for ammunition manufacturers were paying 13 cents a pound for lead bullets. Scavenging was fun and profitable. Many boys, like Albertus McCreary, gathered several hundred pounds each. Apparently the responsibility of entrepreneurism quickly turned tiresome and the boys interest in the battle field debris turned to more adventurous endeavors. According to Albertus: "..every boy had a can of powder hidden with rifles to shoot it in." They would sneak over to Brickyard Lane (now Wainwright Ave.), and: "..load the rifles with the ramrods in and shoot them off." Playing with ordnance left on the field in some instances went beyond fun and turned to tragedy. In the days and months following the battle, there were several incidents of boys being badly injured, even killed, by relic shells unexpectedly exploding. Albertus tells of a school mate who killed himself in this manner: "He found a shell and the contents of shrapnel not coming (out) fast enough, he struck it on a rock, which exploded the shell. He never regained consciousness."[28]

The odyssey of strangers searching for fallen loved ones left behind at Gettysburg was often frustrating and always stressful. It was a sad experience which Gettysburg women often observed first hand while working in the hospitals. Nellie Aughinbaugh was a volunteer nurse and watched this heart wrenching scene play out many times. Two of her many recollections stand out as unique. Occasionally included in the procession of people passing through her hospital looking for relatives or loved ones were southerners who somehow got permission to come through the lines. When they arrived at the hospital they were, "..required to take the oath of allegiance.." before being permitted access. "Some would agree, but others would be most bitter..," and turn away rather than submit to Federal Government coercion and intimidation.[29]

One young woman from a northern state came looking for her sweetheart. She made the rounds of all the hospitals, but to no avail. The obvious conclusion was that her man had been among the many fatally wounded, and was buried in some remote or unidentified grave. In an effort to combat her grief, she elected to stay in Gettysburg and assist with the care of the wounded. She soon became good friends with Nellie. The strain of this work was immense and had worn Nellie down. While assisting a surgeon treat a lung wound, Nellie began to wobble and become light headed. Seeing that she was on the verge of fainting, the surgeon called for an orderly to assist her outside. Passing through the door Nellie handed her basin to her new friend and said: "Go in and help. She went in and the patient was none other than her sweetheart. He lived but a few days longer, but long enough to know her."[30]

The hardships endured by the citizens in the first weeks following the departure of the armies were not limited to physical and emotional stress. They suffered from a drought of formal spiritual renewal. A common complaint found in a number of memoirs was: ". . we have had no Sunday services."[31] This was not a trivial inconvenience for a community where religion was deeply embedded in its culture.

Dr. Henry Baugher, President of Pa. College, held an abbreviated service in the Christ Lutheran Church on the morning of Sunday July 12th. The church was full of wounded so parishioners were not able to attend. That evening the Patriot Daughters serenaded their patients with hymns. Those who were able sang along. The nurses were touched by: "..the sad pathos in the voices of these poor wounded men."[32] That was the only effort to use any church for Sunday services until the wounded were evacuated from the town near the end of the month. Catherine Foster's recollections point out, in a humorous manner, how desperate the situation became in the interim: "For weeks..the scene was a monotonous routine, unbroken by anything to indicate a distinction of days, no Sabbaths and no church bells...a lady had her clothes washed and hung out to dry before she learned it was the Sabbath, and she was a good Presbyterian!"[33]

By the 10th of July there was sufficient food coming into Gettysburg from all over the north so that everybody had enough to eat. Fannie Buehler recalled that friends in New Jersey, Philadelphia and Baltimore were sending, "..barrels of supplies.." to be distributed to the needy: "There was wine, pickles, oranges and lemons, sugar by the barrels, tea and coffee, beef tea, indeed everything that sick (and not sick) people crave or that could give them strength." Clothing also arrived to be distributed: ". . first to the Union soldiers and then to the enemy."[34] It was well that these provisions did arrive because the stream of visitors pouring into town went on unabated and the demand for food was unrelenting.

The overflow of visitors encountered stiff competition for whatever available space could be found for lodging in private homes. Federal officers, wounded too severely to be transported home, were brought into town from field hospitals to be placed in the homes of volunteer citizens. Often an orderly accompanied them to help with the nursing. In these hospitable surroundings they received the necessary care until they recovered sufficiently to travel home for complete convalescence.

Henry and Catherine Garlach agreed to provide room for a Captain Charles Roberts. Roberts was the Adjutant of the 17th Maine Infantry and had his leg amputated after being wounded in the fight at the Wheatfield. Since there were six in the Garlach family and only three small bedrooms, a cot was set up for him in the front parlor; far better accommodations than General Schimmelfennig had enjoyed during his earlier stay with the Garlachs. Robert's remained there for several weeks, and when he had recovered sufficiently to be moved, his father came for him. Captain Roberts never forgot the kindness extended to him by the Garlachs. Following the war, he frequently returned to Gettysburg for GAR reunions and always visited with the family on those occasions.[35]

The James Pierce family opened their house to Col. William Colvill, commander of the 1st Minnesota Infantry and his soldier/nurse. He had been wounded in his shoulder and leg while leading his regiment in a wild charge that resulted in 68% casualties among it's members. Like Roberts, he was nursed back to care over an extended period and was finally able to return home. It was quite natural that strong bonds developed between the wounded and those who worked so devotedly to return them to good health. Tillie recalled the emotional scene when Col. Colvill was finally able to make the trip to his home in St. Paul: "As he was leaving the house he could hardly express fully his thanks and appreciation of our kindness; and on parting kissed us all... We on our part, felt as though one of our own family were leaving." He too came back to visit his benefactors in later years.[36]

Lt. James Purman of the 140th PA. Infantry, also a victim of the Wheatfield fight, was brought to the Samuel Witherow house with a wound in one leg and the other amputated just above the foot. Purman also survived under the tender care ministered by Miss Mary Witherow, Samuel's daughter. In Purman's case the tender care blossomed into love and the two were married not long after his recovery.[37]

Many others were cared for in this manner. Not all of them went on to recovery and a happy ending. When a soldier patient did succumb it was extremely painful for their citizen nurse, who mourned them almost as they would a family member. Sarah Broadhead had two wounded convalescing in her home. As one rapidly slipped towards, "..his long home..," Sarah's diary entry reflected her emotions. The inevitable end: "..adds to my troubles and anxieties.. It is sad; and even we, who have known him so short a time, will miss him."[38]

By the middle of July, the situation at Gettysburg had moved out of the crisis stage and a somewhat orderly routine of town life took over. The streets and been cleaned up, the debris, barricades and dead horses removed. The stench remained as a grim and ugly reminder of what calamitous events had so recently occurred. Again, the Broadhead diary yields a vivid description: "The atmosphere is loaded with the horrid smell of decaying horses and the remains of slaughtered animals, and it is said, from the bodies of men imperfectly buried. I fear we shall be visited with pestilence..." Fortunately that did not happen. Despite the odor and the plaque of flies, huge crowds of visitors still prevailed in town and the demand for lodging was as acute as ever. In her diary entry for July 13th Sarah noted: "The town is as full as ever of strangers.. Twenty are with us tonight (in addition to family and two patients), filling every bed and covering the floors." Others who could not find room stayed on the streets. One who spent the night on a chair in front of a hotel, "..was glad to get even such quarters."[39]

The hospitals began to gain control of their situation. As early as July 10th, Sarah Broadhead commented on the startling improvements she observed at the Seminary hospital in just 48 hours: "I..was rejoiced to see the improvements..Nearly all (patients) have been provided with beds and clean clothing and a more comfortable look pervades the whole building." This was quite remarkable in consideration of the fact that just two days previous, Sarah had discovered a large number of Confederate wounded lying unattended in the rain flooded Seminary basement.(38)

The surgeons in all the hospitals were catching up with the operating load and the presence of ample supplies and outside volunteers to care for the wounded were expediting the improvement of conditions. Daily, large numbers of the wounded were shipped by rail to permanent military hospitals in the cities along the east coast. By late July, the number of wounded still remaining in and around Gettysburg were fewer than 5000, less than 25% of the total originally left behind by the armies. A consolidated General Hospital, named Camp Letterman, was established two miles east of Gettysburg on the York turnpike. All of the remaining wounded, including those in private homes, were moved to the Camp Letterman facility.

By August 1st the ordeal for Gettysburg in caring for the battle's most tragic victims was finally ended. The town was still taxed by the number of outsiders, but as the number of remaining wounded diminished so did the numbers of visitors and volunteers. Things returned so much to normal that the town could once again take comfort in celebrating the Sabbath. L.O. Sloan a delegate to the Christian Commission wrote a letter to a friend in which he commented: "Yesterday (July 19th) was the Holy Sabbath..it was an old fashioned Sunday,..quiet all through town.. and in most all the churches there was (sic) religious services."[41] The churches had been returned at last to their intended purpose.

On the surface the town was scarred; left with those badges of honor on many buildings marking the spot where bullets and shells struck, but did not conquer. In its soul, the town was changed for all time. Little did Jennie McCreary realize the prophesy of her words written to her sister Julia on July 22nd: "..tis' not the same quiet old place as it was..."[42]

What can be said of the behavior of it's citizens throughout the ordeal? Daniel Skelly penned their eulogy in his memoirs: "..the people of Gettysburg assisted in every way..."[43]

What would the response have been if a citizen of that time had been asked: What did you learn from this experience? It is altogether fitting that ten year old Gates Fahnestock, the youngest of those who wrote their reminiscences, be the one to answer for all: "The horrors of war..brought bitter abhorrence of war in itself and as a medium for settling differences."[44]

AFTERWARD:
"The world will little note nor long remember.."

Any chance that the prophesy, contained in this quote from Abraham Lincoln's three minute speech, would apply to Gettysburg, was erased almost before Meade's army had left the field to pursue Lee. Two Gettysburg citizens, David McConaughy and David Wills, were moved to immediate action to insure that the deeds of valor performed on this battlefield by the Federal soldiers would be memorialized. The ultimate consequences of their vision was pure serendipity. They knew that they and their fellow townspeople had just experienced something extraordinary, but it would have been impossible at the time to fully assess what future effect the battle would have on the war, the nation and the world. Henry Jacobs surely was correct in his assessment of everyone's immediate viewpoint of the event when he commented in his memoirs that never, "..did we realize that we were in the midst of one of the greatest battles of modern times."[1] Yet the perseverance of the Federal soldiers, their triumphant entry into town, the pathos of the thousands of wounded, the silent testimony of the dead, the vast wreckage of the field, all combined to stir something in these two men to take action.

Evidence points to David McConaughy as the one who first saw the vision. In his words: "Immediately after the battle...the thought occurred to me that there could be no more fitting and expressive memorial of the heroic valor...of our army...than the battlefield itself." McConaughy was a man of action. Within three weeks of the battle he, "..secured the purchase of the most striking portions of the battle ground..," encompassing the land surrounding the Evergreen Cemetery on Cemetery Hill, East Cemetery Hill, McKnight's Hill (Stevens' Knoll), Little Round Top and the Culp's Hill line.[2] In buying the Cemetery Hill property he enlarged the scope of his vision to include a central burial site for the battle dead. It was McConaughy's plan to inter the dead within the existing cemetery. The land he bought on Cemetery Hill would provide the needed space. If his idea was adopted it would serve to benefit the struggling Evergreen Cemetery Association of which he was president. In a letter to Gov. Curtin on July 25, 1863, he proposed to make: "..the most liberal arrangements..with our Cemetery, for the burial of our own dead..," and the dead of "..all the loyal states, whose sons fell in the glorious strife."[3] On this proposal he would fall short of his vision. A parallel effort to establish a dedicated cemetery for the Union battle dead was already being pushed with the Governor by David Wills and agents for other states. In the end, Evergreen Cemetery would not be the host for the internment of the battle dead.

McConaughy's concept of preserving the battlefield as a memorial did come to fruition. Using his own funds he picked up the purchase options he had negotiated earlier for the key battle sights. In mid-August he addressed a circular to a number of the town's most prominent citizens and proposed forming a Memorial Association to oversee the operation and to expand the battlefield land acquisition. Twenty six citizens answered in the affirmative through a open letter published in the August 19th ADAMS SENTINEL: "We therefore highly approve, and will cheerfully unite in the plan proposed by you..." Within a month the purposes and objectives were formalized and the Gettysburg Battlefield Memorial Association (GBMA) was created. The announcement proclaimed Gettysburg as a battlefield so significant that: "To it all eyes turn as to a sacred spot, which should be guarded with religious care and zealously preserved from disturbance, neglect or decay.. Let it be the shrine to loyalty and patriotism, whither in all times will come the sons of America...to view with wonder and veneration..the sacred scenes...in which were involved the life of the nation and the perpetuity of liberty."[4]

Seldom has a vision proven over time to be so true. However it was not a straight, smooth path for the vision over the years. Although subscription of membership to the GBMA was nationwide, its stewardship was dominated by local citizens. By 1880 it had lost much of its steam and growth was at a standstill. McConaughy, still a driving force in the GBMA, courted the support of the Union veterans through their organization, the Grand Army of the Republic (GAR). In this he was successful, but at a cost of relinquishing control to the GAR. It was a small price to pay to preserve the vision. The GAR generated a new wave of support for the GBMA among its membership. It encouraged the memorialization of the field with the erection of regimental monuments. It utilized it's considerable political clout to pave the way in the U.S. Congress for the establishment of a Gettysburg National Military Park in 1895, that continues today to perpetuate the vision born of a solitary Gettysburg citizen in July 1863.

Congress turned the management of the Park over to the War Department, headed by a three person commission. The first act of the new steward was to expand McConaughy's vision to include all americans who participated in the great battle at Gettysburg. The old Confederate States and their veterans were invited to memorialize their sons and regiments who fought with so much valor on the field. The scope of the Park's land holdings were expanded to include the Confederate battle lines. With this lone act, the Gettysburg National Military Park became a complete and lasting memorial to America's sons and to the strength and endurance of its governing principles. What has not endured is the memory and recognition of the fact that one Gettysburg citizen, David McConaughy, was the genuses of this great shrine.

David Wills is the other Gettysburg citizen given the label of visionary for his role in generating the concept of establishing a Soldiers National Cemetery to honor the Union dead at Gettysburg. Labeling him a visionary might be an overstatement, but he certainly was a man who recognized a good idea when he saw one, and had the drive to follow through with it. Wills wrote Governor Curtin on July 24th proposing a concept whereby the State of Pennsylvania would buy, "..a common burial ground for the dead.." in which all the fallen still on the field would be interred: "It is my idea for Pennsylvania to purchase the ground at once.. The other states would certainly... contribute towards defraying the expenses..." Wills went on to say that his idea had the endorsement of New York Governor Seymour's brother and "others." This letter started a chain of events which led to the creation of the Soldiers National Cemetery.[5]

The simple statement that "it is my idea" has credited Wills as the father of the Soldiers National Cemetery. There is evidence that challenges Wills' ownership of the idea and the vision. Dr. Theodore S. Dimon of New York was at Gettysburg shortly after the fighting ceased, in an official capacity to look after the State's wounded and dead. The states other than Pennsylvania had a problem of handling their dead. Pennsylvania was paying for the expense of returning each of her deceased native sons to their home towns for final interment. The expense of matching this gesture was prohibitive for the more distant states. Dimon recorded in his report dated August 1st, the substance of a meeting of various state agents, including David Wills, held before July 25th to discuss the problem of what to do, over the long run, with the dead on the field. It was Dr. Dimon's claim that: "At this meeting I presented a proposition that a portion of the ground...on Cemetery Hill should be purchased for a permanent burial place for the soldiers..The proposition met with approval...Mr. Wills entered into negotiations for the purchase of the land." If the veracity of Dr. Dimon is accepted he, not David Wills, is the true father of the Soldiers National Cemetery.[6]

At the very least David Wills can be credited with being the implementor. He ran with the idea and was the primary force in bringing it to fruition. Wills became Governor Curtin's designated agent in Gettysburg to manage the project. In this role he found himself embroiled in a confrontation with David McConaughy. McConaughy had acquired the ground that was desired by the states for the placement of the Soldiers National Cemetery. He had a vision in which the dead would be buried in the Evergreen Cemetery and he had bought the land to insure adequate acreage. Once realizing that the Governor favored a dedicated cemetery site over interring the dead in Evergreen, McConaughy offered to sell the land to the state at cost. McConaughy corresponded directly with Gov. Curtin rather than through Wills. Wills responded to this obvious slight by contradicting McConaughy. He notified the Governor that McConaughy's land was only for sale at a speculator's price, and recommended to Curtin that an alternate site be purchased on the "left center" of the line (probably where the old Visitors Center and the Cyclorama buildings now reside) for a price of $200 per acre. This was the same price quoted by McConaughy for the site on Cemetery Hill. Curtin was confused and frustrated by the contradictions concerning price and site recommendations and apparently enlisted the aid of two prominent Gettysburg citizens, David Buehler and Edward Fahnestock, to mediate a resolution.

Although practically neighbors and fellow members of the Bar in Gettysburg, Wills and McConaughy had some sort of barrier between them. They would not communicate directly with each other. Buehler and Fahnestock, mutual friends of both parties successfully bridged the gap. In short order, the site issue was resolved and the purchase of the McConaughy property by the State of Pennsylvania finalized.

Once beyond the site hurdle, Wills rapidly and efficiently moved the project from a plan to a reality. He contracted with William Saunders, noted landscape architect from Washington D. C., to lay out the design. He arranged for the gathering of the bodies and re-interment within the new cemetery. He conceived the idea of a grand dedication ceremony. Finally, it was David Wills, although maybe only as an after thought, who initiated the invitation that brought Abraham Lincoln to Gettysburg to deliver, "..a few appropriate remarks.." at the dedication of the cemetery.

The date for the dedication ceremony was set for November 19, 1863, four and one half months after the great battle had ended. Once again, Gettysburg faced a great invasion of humanity. This time they were expecting it, and they took the pains to prepare. Harvey Sweney left a clear description of the preparations: "Our old town roused up to action." Meetings were held to plan for food and lodging. "Churches, public schools, town halls, all the private dwellings, barns, etc., were thrown open to receive them." By the week of the event: "..every house groaned with.. good things.. to feed the coming crowd."[7]

The crowd that gathered in Gettysburg to witness the ceremony was estimated to be between fifteen and twenty thousand, most of whom were in town for the night of November 18th. Lincoln and his party arrived by train around 6 P.M.. The crowd was in a festive mood, fueled by the abundance of dignitaries and bands playing patriotic songs. The weather was unusually mild for that time of year and the street party lasted well into the wee hours of the morning. A big factor in keeping people on the streets all night was the fact that many could find no accommodations, and they simply had no place to which they could retire. Despite the best of plans there was simply not enough rooms to meet the demand. Even William Saunders, the man who designed the physical layout of the cemetery to be dedicated and a honored guest at the ceremony, had to settle for a chair in a crowded parlor as a substitute for a bed.[8]

The next day was glorious. The un-seasonal weather prevailed with sunshine and the temperature, "..almost balmy." At 10 A.M. the procession began to form along all four streets leading into the square. Lincoln emerged from David Wills' house and mounted his assigned horse. The mount had been supplied by Col. John Mc-Clellan, brother of the proprietor of the McClellan House. The horse was selected because it was not very spirited, and the President had a reputation of being, "..not one of the best horsemen."[9]

Daniel Skelly along with his boyhood chum, J.C. Felty, watched the preparations from a vantage point in front of the McClellan House. Skelly described the President: "..the most peculiar looking figure on horseback I had ever seen. He rode a medium sized black horse and was dressed in black and wore a black high silk hat. It seemed to me that his feet almost touched the ground, but he was perfectly at ease.."[10]

Several other youngsters, besides Skelly and Felty, watched the happenings from nearby. Liberty Hollinger and some friends were in the home of Robert McCreary, immediately across York Street from David Wills' house, watching the parade get under way. Liberty remembered: " ..on the front steps of Judge Will's home Governor Curtin and some others were greeting the people as they passed, shaking hands, joking ..having a jolly good time generally." Then she saw the President: "The chief impression made on me...was the inexpressible sadness on his face, which was in so marked contrast with what was going on...where all was excitement and where everyone was having such a jolly time." She noted that about half the crowd at the Wills house and in the square had departed for the Cemetery before Lincoln finally made his appearance. Like Skelly, she remembered that the President's, "..feet almost touched the ground.." when he was seated on his horse. Then it was time to begin. At this point, Liberty recalled that the President's steed made a move that served to brighten Mr. Lincoln's mood: "When the band began to play the President's horse began to prance around. It seemed to amuse the President and then that solemn faced man actually smiled."[11]

The procession was substantial in size; consisting of a cavalry unit, two infantry units, two military bands, local and state dignitaries and the President with his entourage. When it got under way shortly after 11 A.M., moving south along Baltimore Street, it was described by eye witnesses as "beautiful" and "solemn." Harvey Sweney watched from his front stoop and recalled it as, "..a living sea of human beings;" phraseology hauntingly reminiscent of the language used by Anna Garlach to describe another crowded procession down Baltimore Street on the afternoon of July 1st.[12] The crowd seemed to take some humor from the spectacle of the President on his too short horse. For many, particularly relatives of those who were about to be honored, it was not a day to joke and laugh. The President's mood was in keeping with the purpose of the ceremony. Daniel Skelly felt the President's face, "..lined and sad, bore traces of the tremendous worry the ordeal of the war had brought to him." H.C. Holloway, a student at the Pennsylvania College, was touched by the "..great melancholy.." that settled on the President's "..countenance."[13]

Parade along Baltimore St., Nov. 19, 1863, to the Soldiers National Cemetary. (GNMP)

When the head of the procession reached the fork created by the intersection of the Emmitsburg Road with Baltimore Street, it turned into the former and headed towards the Taneytown Road. The crowd of spectators took the shortest route to the speakers platform by continuing straight on Baltimore Street up the hill to the main entrance to the Soldiers National Cemetery. The procession, meanwhile, turned left onto the Taneytown Road and continued until it reached a point almost adjacent to today's rear entrance to the Cemetery. Turning left again, it proceeded to the platform, set on a high point of ground behind or south of the site of the Soldiers National Monument.[14] Edward Everett, the principal orator for the occasion, was already there, awaiting the arrival of the others. After the dignitaries were in place on the platform the proceedings began.[15]

A little more than two hours elapsed while Edward Everett delivered his oration. When he finally sat down it was Lincoln's turn to deliver his, "..appropriate remarks." Henry Jacobs was standing close by and studied the President closely while Ward Lamon introduced Lincoln to the crowd. He noticed, "..slight nervousness in his bearing..," as he prepared himself to deliver the words that would forever link his name with the little town of Gettysburg, and help lift him into the rarified heights of immortality. But first were the simple gestures of preparation, as recalled by Jacobs: "He reached in his side pocket and drew out an old fashioned metal spectacles case. He put a low pair of glasses before his eyes. Then reaching again into his pocket he drew out a sheet of paper, considerably crumpled. Then he arose, with his glasses at the tip of his nose."[16]

Abraham Lincoln stepped forward to the speakers rostrum. In his clear, high pitched voice, he slowly spoke the words that described the purpose of the war in ideological terms and redefined for the people the spirit and intent of the nation's very foundation. The speech lasted less than three minutes. The words and their message would live on, forever.[17]

For many in the audience that day, the President's speech seemed to end before it got started. They were startled by the brevity and paused waiting for more. When it became clear that he was finished the crowd belatedly responded. H.C. Holloway remembered: "..the applause was most hearty, rising like the sound of many waters."[18] When the ceremonies were completed, Lincoln once more demonstrated a lack of appreciation of the durability of his words. In the text of his address, he predicted: "The world will little note nor long remember what we say here..," a gross miscalculation. When his Attorney General, Wayne McVeagh, grasped his hand and remarked: "You have made an immortal address!" Lincoln responded quickly, and perhaps over modestly: "Oh, you must not say that. You must not be extravagant about it."[19]

Quickly the President returned to the reality of the moment and like any good politician took the opportunity to work the crowd. Taking advantage of the natural confusion that temporarily prevailed on the platform, he approached Mrs. Edward Fahnestock. Extending his hand, he commented that he could not help noticing her during the ceremony and was convinced that he had met her before. The flattered Marie Fahnestock assured him that now was their first meeting.(20) Descending the stairs from the platform his eyes came into contact with those of a young girl. Lincoln held out his hand and said: "Hello, young lady , who are you?" The girl took his hand and replied: "I am Mary Elizabeth (Montfort)." With that simple gesture Abraham Lincoln provided a young Gettysburg girl with, ". . the greatest moment of my life." It was a memory that transcended the nightmares suffered during those days just a few months before, which included the mortal wounding of her father.[21]

There would be an opportunity for more interaction with the `common people.' Upon returning to Wills' house the President had a short interval of time before going out again amongst the crowd to attend a short political rally at the Presby-

terian Church featuring an address by Governor David Tod of Ohio. He took the opportunity to send for local hero John Burns to accompany him. When Burns arrived at the front door the President greeted him and the two walked together up the center of Baltimore Street to the church. Once in the crowded sanctuary Burns and Lincoln sat side by side in a pew until the political speeches were done. Albertus McCreary was one of many crammed into the church and found himself along the aisle as the president and his party moved toward the exit. Not one to let such an opportunity pass he stuck out his hand and asked:
"Mr. Lincoln, will you shake hands with me?"

"Certainly," was the response.

Albertus would proudly remember for the rest of his life that Abraham Lincoln, "..gave me a good strong grasp."[23]

From the steps of the church the procession moved to the train station, where the president's cars awaited. A final wave to the crowd, and he was gone. In less than two years Abraham Lincoln would have moved on to take his proper place with "the Ages." The war would have ended, and the nation would have reunited, forever.

Perhaps the viability of the concept of reuniting the north and south was symbolically demonstrated in Gettysburg not long after the Soldier's National Cemetery dedication ceremonies. Liberty Hollinger left us with this plain, but meaningful anecdote: "Many romances were developed during the stay of the soldiers. One of our most intimate friends (a northerner) married a southerner who her mother had nursed back to health."[24] Enemies no more; just Americans.

APPENDIX

WHERE THE 1863 GETTYSBURG CIVILIANS LIVED

The following is a table, by street, of the location of the residences of 1863 civilians and significant buildings cited in the text of this book. Where it is known, the citizen's occupation is listed. All street address numbers are contemporary Borough assignments. When a exact site address is not known for certain, or the site is now incorporated into another property, it is designated with (*) in place of a #. The main sources for the data contained in this appendix are deed records on file in the Adams County Courthouse; the 1860 U.S. Gettysburg Borough Census, historic photographs of the Borough of Gettysburg, the 1858 and 1872 Adams County Maps, the Sanborne Map Co. Fire Insurance Maps of Gettysburg and the Historic Building Survey Committee reports, all on file at the Adams County Historical Society.

BALTIMORE STREET (west side):

- John L. Schick's Store: #1.
    Served as the supply distribution headquarters for the Christian Commission. The store occupied the north 1/2 of the 1st floor of the Stoever building. Today it is the site of The House of Bender.

- Martin L. Stoever family: #3.
    Professor at The Pennsylvania College. The original ca. 1814 building remains with only minor external alterations to it's 1863 appearance. Located on the south side of the S.W. quadrant of the square and Baltimore Street.
    . Elizabeth McConaughy Stoever: Wife/mother.

- William Guinn family: #9-11.
    Site is located between the Martin Stoever and Moses McClean buildings. In 1863 the building was owned by Hannah McClean and leased to the Guinn family. The original building was razed and replaced with the current structure ca. 1900. Today it is part of the hardware store located at #13.

- Moses McClean family: #13.
    Attorney at Law. Building served as his office and residence. The original structure has been altered by adding a 3rd story and a new front facade. Today it

is a hardware store and apartments.
. Hannah McClean: Wife/mother.
. Robert McClean: Son.
. Elizabeth McClean: Daughter
. Colin McClean: Son

- Fahnestock Brothers Store: #47.
Located at the N.W. corner of Baltimore and W. Middle Streets. The original building exists within the current, expanded and much altered, structure. Today's building does not resemble the 1863 structure in appearance.

- Edward G. Fahnestock:
Merchant and owner/partner in Fahnestock Bros.. Lived in the north 1/2 of the Fahnestock store building with his wife and widowed mother.
. Marie Fahnestock: wife/mother.

- Adams County Courthouse:
Located at the S.W. corner of Baltimore and W. Middle Streets. Served as a Hospital. The original building exists with a 1909 "T" addition to the rear. A modern courthouse located on the south side of the original building now serves the county.

- Daniel Culp: (*).
Cabinetmaker. House/shop site now occupied by the new courthouse.

- David McCreary family: (*),
Saddle and harness maker. House site was located at the S.W. corner of Baltimore and High Streets. House and shop buildings razed ca. 1890. Site now occupied by The Prince of Peace Episcopal Church.
. Albertus McCreary: Son.

- Dr. John Runkel family: #231.
Physician. Original house remains with only roof dormers and an addition to the rear compromising its 1863 appearance.

- James Pierce: #303.
Butcher. Original house remains with modest alterations to 1863 appearance.
. Tillie Pierce: Daughter.

- George Schriver family: #311.

Sgt. in Cole's Union cavalry company (not present during the battle at Gettysburg). Original house remains with recent restoration to its 1863 appearance. The south end of the garret was heavily used by Confederate sharpshooters.

. Henrietta Weikert Schriver: Wife/mother.

- Henry Garlach family: #323.

Cabinetmaker. Original house remains with only minor modification. The old cabinet shop portion of the building was converted into two house units(#321 & #319) ca. 1893.

. Catherine Garlach: Wife/mother.
. Anna Garlach: Daughter.
. Will Garlach: Son.
. Francis Garlach: Infant son.

- Harvey Sweney family: #401.

The original brick building still stands with negligible external alteration. Post war additions were made to the rear. Numerous bullet scars are visible on the south wall in the vicinity of the garret window used by Confederate sharpshooters.

. Catherine Sweney: wife/mother.
. Lizzie Sweney: Daughter.

- Henry Rupp family: #451.

Tanner. Wartime brick building was razed shortly after the end of the war. The existing clapboard building was erected on the original house site in 1869.

- The Wagon Hotel.

This busy hotel site was located just south of the fork created by the intersection of Baltimore Street and the Emmitsburg Road. The original was replaced by a modern hotel facility prior to 1900. The newer building gave way to a service station after WWII. The site is now occupied by a Sheetz convenience store.

BALTIMORE STREET (east side):

- William A. Duncan: #24-26.

Attorney at Law. This site was his residence. Original building has been razed and replaced with the current structure.

- James Fahnestock family: #48.

Merchant and owner/partner in Fahnestock Bros.. The building is located at the N.E. corner of Baltimore and E. Middle Streets. The original house still exists although much altered from its 1863 appearance by modifications that added a 3rd story and created a store front on the 1st floor.
. Sarah Fahnestock: Wife/mother.
. Gates Fahnestock: Son.

- John Cannon: #100.
Marble cutter. Building was located on the S.E. corner of Baltimore and E. Middle Streets. Cannon probably rented the house. He operated a marble cutting yard to the rear in which Confederate General Jubal Early established his Hqs. on July 2nd. The Deed shows the property under the joint ownership of the Dr. David Horner heirs (Drs. Robert and Charles) and David Kendlehart in 1863. The original building(s) no longer exist.

- David Kendlehart family: #110.
Shoemaker, Attorney at Law and President of the Borough Council. The original building stands with restored front facade.
. Margaretta Kendlehart: Daughter.

- David Buehler family: #112.
Attorney at Law and U.S. Postmaster. The original three story house remains. Front facade has been restored within the past thirty years.
. Fannie Buehler: wife/mother.

- THE COMPILER Building: #126.
The original clapboard building was razed sometime prior to 1900 to make room for the brick building currently standing on the site.

- Henry Stahle: (*).
Editor of THE COMPILER. Site of his house is now the northern end of the County Library property. It adjoined the old COMPILER building at 126 Baltimore Street. The building was razed in 1912 to make room for the construction of the U.S. Post Office Building (now the County Library). This building was the site of the emergency treatment of Col. William W. Dudley's leg on the evening of July 1st.

- The Presbyterian Church:

The building is located on S.E. corner of Baltimore and E. High Streets. It served as a hospital. The 1863 church building was completely dismantled and replaced with the current structure in 1963. The only original part of the structure reused were the great wooden ceiling beams.

- Agnes Barr family: #220.

The 1863 building is still on the site, having been modified and enlarged with a 3rd floor and rear addition ca. 1930.

- Ann C. McCurdy: #224.

Charles McCurdy's grandmother. The house, severely modified with enlargements and facade restructure, remains incorporated in the current structure. It was originally a double house with the south half serving for years (1885 until her death in the 1922) as the post war residence of Salome Myers Stewart. The Stewart portion was razed in 1980s and replaced with the south wing currently attached to #224.

- Samuel Witherow family: #302.

Auctioneer. The 1863 house with only minor alterations to the front facade still stands.

. Mary Witherow: Daughter/nurse. Married her post battle patient, Lt. Purman.

- Rev. George Bergstresser family: #304.

Methodist minister. The 1863 building exists today, but with major alterations. The front facade was removed ca. 1910 and replaced with the one which exists today. An artillery shell has been placed in the wall at approximately the spot where one entered in 1863, badly frightening, but not harming daughter, Laura.

. Laura Bergstresser: Daughter.

- John Winebrenner family: #404.

Tanner. Original house remains virtually unchanged from it's 1863 appearance.

.M.L. Culler: Seminary student and guest, July 1-3.

- Samuel McCreary family: (*).

Brick maker. The house no longer stands. It was razed ca. 1951 by the Gettysburg School Board and the site is now the southern half of the school complex entrance area at the intersection of Lefever and Baltimore Streets. The 1863 house was identical in design to the John Winebrenner house still standing to the north, across Lefever Street. The house site was just behind the huge Sycamore tree standing on the entrance area lawn.

- Louis McClellan family: #518.

Laborer. The original, double brick building still stands. Today it houses the Jennie Wade Museum. In 1863 it was the site of the accidental death and initial burial location (back yard) of Jennie Wade.

. Georgia Wade McClellan: Wife, and older sister of Jennie Wade.

CHAMBERSBURG STREET (SOUTH SIDE):

- Smith S. McCreary family: #22.

Hat maker. The 1863 building still stands, but much modified over the years to accommodate commercial use of the 1st floor. The modifications included the addition of a full 3rd floor.

. Jennie McCreary: daughter.

- Robert McCurdy family: #26.

President of the Gettysburg Rail Road. The 1863 building was radically modified ca.1900. Major portions of the original building are contained in the existing one.

. Charles McCurdy: Son.

- Christ Lutheran Church: #30.

Hospital. Original building remains intact with new rear addition.

- Sarah Jane Weikert: #46.

Boarding House. 1863 structure exists with 3rd floor added ca. 1900.

- Samuel Herbst: #54-58.

Agent for Manny's Reaper. The 1863 building no longer exists.

- Dr. Henry S. Huber: #60.

Physician. The 1863 building still exists with considerable modification reflecting commercial utilization over the years. It served as Huber's office and residence.

- Alexander Cobean: #102-04.

Hat and shoe merchant. Original house razed and replaced with the existing structure in 1916.

- William Boyer family: #214. Merchant.

The site was Boyer's residence. The 1863 building was razed and replaced with the existing building after 1900.

- Charles Tyson and wife: #216.

Photographer. The original building still exists, having been modified by additions and a false brick, front facade. This site was Tyson's residence.

. Maria Tyson: wife.

- John Burns and wife: #252-54.

Retired constable and War of 1812 veteran. The 1863 structure was razed and replaced with the current building ca 1890.

CHAMBERSBURG STREET (NORTH SIDE):

- Alexander Buehler: #9.

Druggist. The site was both his store and residence. The original building is incorporated in the structure that exists today. Alterations that added a 3rd story were made ca. 1890.

- David McConaughy family: #11.

Attorney at Law. Site of his office and residence. Except for the 1st floor facade the original building is incorporated in the current structure. This building had a 3rd story added ca. 1890.

- Philip "Petey" Winters: #13.

Baker. Site of his bakery shop and residence. The original building was razed and replaced by the existing structure ca.1885. First home of the Gettysburg Military Park commission.

- Belle King family: #41.

Wife/housekeeper. The 1863 building was a two story, side gabled roof, Federal style, structure. It underwent massive alterations in 1868 and again in the first decade of this century when the Tudor style facade was added.

- John Scott family: #43-45.

Merchant. Original house still exists, modified by the addition of a 3rd story. The 1863 telegraph office was in this building, also a general merchandise store.

. Martha Scott: Wife.

. Hugh Scott: Son/Telegraph operator.

. Mary Scott: daughter

. Mary McAllister: Sister-in-law/merchant.

- Dr. Charles Horner family: #47.

Physician. Site of his residence and office. The 1863 building was razed in 1903 and replaced with the existing building.

. Caroline Horner: Wife/mother.

- Dr. Robert Horner family: #51.

Physician. The original house, which once belonged to Thaddeus Stevens, noted wartime Radical Republican, was razed in 1923. In 1863 the building served as his residence and drug store.

. Mary Horner: Wife/mother.

- Nancy Weikert: #55.

Widow. The 1863 building was razed and replaced with the existing structure ca. 1890.

- Jacob Gilbert and wife: #213.

Part of a group of four connected houses known as 'Warren's Row'. The entire row exists today and appears about as it did in 1863.

. Elizabeth Gilbert: Wife/mother.

- Joseph Broadhead family: #217.

R.R. Express messenger. The Broadheads occupied the western end-house of 'Warren's Row'. The 1863 building still exists in much it's 1863 appearance.

. Sarah Broadhead: Wife/mother.

_ David Troxel Sr.: #219.

Harness maker. The 1863 structure exists with front addition.

YORK STREET (SOUTH SIDE):

- David Wills family: #1.

Attorney at Law. The house which served as Will's office and residence is located on the S.E. corner of the square. The original building has been restored to approximate it's period appearance. President Lincoln resided at this house during his November 1863 visit to participate in the dedication of the Soldiers National Cemetery.

- Charles Tyson's photography studio: #9. 1863 building still exists.

- Valentine Sauppee family: #35.

Baker. The building contained Sauppee's residence and bakery. A large portion of the 1863 structure is incorporated in the existing building, although modifications have dramatically changed the exterior and interior appearance.

- St. James Lutheran Church:

It served as a hospital. Located at the S.E. corner of York and Stratton Streets. The 1863 building was razed in 1911 and replaced with the present structure in 1912.

-Sarah Montfort family: (*).

House site is now a parking area on the west side of the old fire hall building, located at the S.W. corner of York and Liberty Streets. Sarah King lived at the corner lot and in her reminiscence, printed in THE COMPILER (July 4th, 1906), she said she lived two doors east of the Montfort's house.

. Mary Elizabeth Montfort: daughter.

. Jennie Ann: daughter.

- Sarah King family: (*).

The house was located S.W. corner of York and Liberty Streets. The site is now part of large building which until 1991 housed the Gettysburg Fire Department. The 1863 house structure was razed many years ago.

- Jacob Hollinger (*).

Merchant. (Whose warehouse stood at S.E. corner of Stratton and railroad tracks). The house and barn were located in the triangle formed by the junction of York and Hanover Streets. The 1863 brick farm house fronted on York Street. The barn and sheds were on the Hanover Street side. The buildings were razed years ago, to make room for the high school building erected on the site in 1909.

. Liberty Hollinger: daughter.

. Julia Hollinger: daughter.

YORK STREET (NORTH SIDE):

- Robert G. McCreary: (*)2.

Attorney at Law. Site of McCreary's two story brick dwelling is now incorporated in the building that occupies the east side of the N.E. quadrant of the square. It stood between it's current host building and the Gettysburg Bank (now PNC Bank). It was razed ca. 1902.

- Gettysburg Bank (now PNC): #10. The 1863 building was razed years ago. Today the modern bank structure occupies a significant portion of the block, encompassing the sites of the wartime Bank building, Carson house, the Globe Inn and Joseph Gillespie's grocery store.

- T. Duncan Carson family: (*).
   Teller at the Gettysburg Bank. The house site is now part of the PNC Bank complex.
   . Mary Carson: wife.

- The Globe Inn: (*).
   The site is now incorporated into the existing PNC Bank building. The wartime Inn was a 2 story, brick structure with a front balcony.
   . Charles Will: proprietor.
   . John Will: son.

- Joseph Gillespie's Grocery Store: (*).
   The site is now incorporated into the east end of the PNC Bank grounds.

CARLISLE STREET:

- Washington Hotel: #32.
   The hotel building was razed and is now the site of the Lincoln Diner.

- Gettysburg R.R. Station: #35.
   The 1863 station building exists today with very little modification of appearance. Today it serves as a tourist information center for the Travel Council.

- Jacob Aughinbaugh family: #104.
   Coach maker. 1863 2 story building no longer existing, replaced ca. 1900 with current structure. Actual site of family in 1863 residence is not known for certain. Nellie's reminiscence suggests that it was on Carlisle Street, adjoining her uncle's "large store". The 1863 tax records show Jacob as not owning property. They apparently rented a house from George Arnold adjoining Spangler's produce warehouse property on the South. Aughinbaugh had previously owned this property.

. Anna Margret Aughinbaugh.: Wife/mother.
. Nellie Aughinbaugh: Daughter/ milliner.

- John L Schick family: #125
Original 1863 structure no longer stands, being replaced with Monahan Funeral Home. In his reminiscence published in the PHILADELPHIA NORTH AMERICAN, July 7, 1909, he tells of sitting out the battle in the cellar of his home and smoking "21 cigars" a day.

W. MIDDLE STREET (NORTH SIDE):

- Harvey Wattles family: #48.
Businessman. The 1863 building no longer exists. Washington St. South side.

- James Bowen: (*)43.
The 1863 building no longer exists.

- Johnston Skelly family: (*)47.
Skelly rented his residence from James Bowen, a next door neighbor. The 1863 building no longer exists.
. Daniel Skelly: Clerk for Fahnestock Bros.

- George Little family: #55.
Merchant. The 1863 building still exists. It has been altered with a rear addition and a front bay window.

- Elizabeth Minnigh family: #69.
Wife/mother. The house on the N.E. corner of W. Middle and S. Washington Streets has been extensively modified, but still exists. The 3rd story, mansard roof, rear addition and commercial front are all post 1863 alterations. The house that occupies the old yard/garden on the east side of the Minnigh house was built ca. 1873. Her son, Henry, commanded Company K, 30th PA. Infantry, an Adams County unit in the 3rd Division, 5th Corps, Army of the Potomac. They fought at Little Round Top on the evening of July 2nd.

- Michael Jacobs family: #103.
Professor at The Pennsylvania College. The 1863 building at the N.W. corner of W. Middle and S. Washington Streets, still exists. It has a post battle rear addition. Otherwise it retains its original exterior appearance.

. Henry Eyster Jacobs: Son and student at The Pennsylvania College (later a Lutheran minister).
. Julia Jacobs: Daughter.

- Hiram Warren: (*)237-239.
   Moulder. The site of the Warren house now occupies the west side of present day Kennie's Market. The original structure has been razed.
   . Mary Warren (Fastnacht): Daughter.

W. MIDDLE STREET (SOUTH SIDE):

- Henry Fahnestock family: #70.
   Merchant and owner/partner of Fahnestock Bros. The 1863 house, located on the S.E. corner of W. Middle and S. Washington streets, remains although in a much altered condition.
H. D. Wattles

E. MIDDLE STREET (NORTH SIDE):

- William McClean family: #22.
   Attorney at Law. McLean's 1863 house still stands, although alterations to the rear have enlarged it considerably. It is the east half of a two story, brick, double house.
   . Fannie McClean: Wife/mother.
   . Hannah Mary McClean: Daughter.
   . Olivia McClean: Daughter.

E. MIDDLE STREET (SOUTH SIDE):

- Methodist Church: #55. (Also Gar Hall Post #9. 1882-1933).
   The 1863 building remains with some additions to the rear of the building.

THE "DIAMOND" OR SQUARE:

- William Duncan Law Office: (*)9.
   The 1863 building located along the west side of the N.W. quadrant of the square no longer stands. The existing building replaced it prior to 1900.

- The McClellan House:

The 1863 building, located on the north side of the N.E. quadrant, no longer exists (Some small portions of the original foundations may still exist). Now known as the Gettysburg Hotel. It might have been referred to by its earlier name, the Franklin House, in some 1863 accounts.

-Robert Harper: (*)10 (S.E. quadrant).

Printer/editor/publisher. The two story brick building was Harper's residence. Next door was the office for THE ADAMS SENTINEL. Both 1863 structures were demolished before 1900 and replaced with the existing building.

W. HIGH STREET (NORTH SIDE):

- St. Francis Xavier Catholic Church: (*)45.

Hospital. Despite a significant fire in the 1893 most of the 1863 exterior is incorporated in the existing structure. The current pillars and pediment were not part of the wartime building.

- Peter Myers family: #55.

Justice of the Peace. The 1863 structure exists today with very little change in appearance. The Myers family rented this property from John Plank.
  . Salome Myers: Daughter and school teacher.
  . Sue Myers: Daughter, student.

- Solomon Powers family: #63.

Granite cutter. The 1863 house structure still exists.
  . Catherine Powers: wife/mother
  . Alice Powers: daughter

W. HIGH STREET (SOUTHSIDE):

- The United Presbyterian Church: (*)75.

Hospital. (not to be confused with the Presbyterian Church located on Baltimore St. at E. High St.) The 1863 structure stood just west of the David McCreary property. It was razed ca. 1890. Modern structures exist on the site today, housing the Methodist church complex.

- Eyster's, Young Ladies Seminary: #66-68.

It was a "finishing school" for girls in 1863. This original building and surrounding property stands on the S.E. corner of W. High and S. Washington Streets. Built ca.1813, the building appears today much as it did in 1863.

. Rebecca Eyster: Widow/proprietor/teacher.

E. HIGH STREET (NORTH SIDE):

- Gettysburg Public High School: #40.

Built in 1858 as the town's first consolidated public school building. The exterior of the building remains practically unchanged with the exception of the dismantled bell cupola. The bell still exists and is the property of the Gettysburg Area School District on display in Alumni Park, Baltimore and LeFever Sts.

- The German Reformed Church:

Hospital. Located at the N.W. corner of E. High and S. Stratton Streets. The majority of the 1863 building is incorporated into the existing structure.

BRECKENRIDGE STREET (NORTH SIDE):

-Mary Wade family: #52.

Seamstress/tailor. The 1863 building still exists but in a highly altered appearance. Post war modifications included a second story and side additions.

. Mary Virginia "Jennie" Wade: Daughter/seamstress.

. Sam Wade: son (lived and worked at the James Pierce's).

S. WASHINGTON STREET (WEST SIDE):

- James Foster family: #155.

Retired. Located on the N.E. corner of S. Washington and W. High Streets, the 1863 building remains virtually unchanged from its wartime appearance.

. Catherine Foster: Daughter.

. Belle Stewart: Cousin and student at the Eyster's Young Ladies Seminary.

. Catherine Foster: wife /mother

RAILROAD STREET (SOUTH SIDE):

- David Warren: (*).

The house building no longer exists. The site is now part of a parking lot adjoining (on the east) a group of stores across the street from the current Southern States property.

. Elizabeth Warren: Wife /mother.

. Leander Warren: Son.

PENNSYLVANIA (GETTYSBURG) COLLEGE CAMPUS:

- Henry L. Baugher D.D., President Pa. College:

President's House. The building still stands on the campus, one of two wartime buildings that survive to this day (Pennsylvania Hall or "Old Dorm" is the other survivor).

. Clara Mary Baugher: Wife/mother.

LUTHERAN THEOLOGICAL SEMINARY BUILDING:

- Emanuel Ziegler family:

Caretaker. The Ziegler family occupied an apartment on the first or ground floor of the Seminary Building. The building survives today in nearly its wartime appearance. It is currently home to the Adams County Historical Society.

. Lydia Catherine Ziegler (Clare): Daughter.

OAK RIDGE SEMINARY:

- Carrie Sheads: #331 Buford Ave. (Chambersburg Pike).

Teacher. The building which served as residence and school still stands, with only the addition of dormers to the roof to alter its 1863 external appearance. It was used as a hospital during and following the battle.

S.W. CORNER OF WEST AND SPRINGS STREETS:

- Anthony Sellinger Family:

. Anthony.

. Catherine.

. Mary age 13.

. Michael age 10.

Rented house which stood where the Dollar Store now stands in the Gettysburg Shopping Center.

BIBLIOGRAPHY

Books:
-Alleman, Tillie Pierce. At Gettysburg, or What a Young Girl Saw and Heard of the Battle. W. Lake Borland, NY, NY. 1889.
-Bloom, Robert A. A History of Adams County Pa. 1700-1990. ACHS Publisher, Gettysburg, Pa. 1992.
-Busey, John W. & Martin, David G. Regimental Strengths and Losses at Gettysburg. Longstreet House, Highstown, NJ. 1986.
-Coco, Gregory A. On a Bloodstained Field II. Thomas Publications, Gettysburg, Pa. 1989.
-Coco, Gregory A. War Stories. Thomas Publications, Gettysburg, Pa. 1989.
-Coco, Gregory A. A Vast Sea of Misery. Thomas Publications, Gettysburg, Pa. 1989.
-Hancock, Cornelia. The South After Gettysburg: Letters of Cornelia Hancock. Edited by Henrietta S. Jaquette, University Press, Philadelphia, Pa. 1937.
-Herdegen, Lance & Beaudot, Wm. J.K. In the Bloody Railroad Cut at Gettysburg. Morningside House Inc., Dayton, Ohio. 1990.
-The Patriot Daughters of Lancaster. Hospital Scenes After the Battle of Gettysburg. Henry B. Ashmead, Philadelphia, Pa. 1864. Reprinted by G. Graig Caba. 1993.
-Jacobs Michael. The Rebel Invasion of Maryland and Pennsylvania and the Battle of Gettysburg. J. B. Lippincott & Co. Philadelphia, Pa. 1864.
-McCurdy Charles. M. A. Memoir. Reed & Witting Co., Pittsburgh, Pa. 1929.
-Moore, Frank. Women of the War. S. S. Scranton Co. Hartford, Connecticut. 1866.
-Skelly, Daniel A. A Boy's Experience During the Battle of Gettysburg. Privately published, Gettysburg, Pa. 1932.
-Small, Cindy L. The Jennie Wade Story. Thomas publications, Gettysburg, Pa. 1991.
-Umrau, Harlan D. Administrative History, GNMP and the National Cemetery. U.S. Dept. of The Interior. 1991.
-Wills, Garry. Lincoln at Gettysburg. Simon & Schuster NY. 1992.

Pamphlets and Periodicals:
-Aughinbaugh, Nellie. Personal Experiences of a Young Girl During the Battle of Gettysburg. Privately printed 1941. On file at ACHS.
-Battlefield Journals. "Like Angel's Wings", The Sisters of Charity. Battlefield Journals, publisher, Mercersburg, Pa. 1999.
-Broadhead, Sarah. A Diary of a Lady of Gettysburg. Privately printed. Covers June 14th through July 14th. On file at ACHS.
-Hollinger, Liberty (Glutz). Some Personal Recollections of the Battle of Gettysburg. Privately printed 1925. On file at ACHS.
-Jacobs, Henry E. Gettysburg Fifty Years Ago, 'The Lutheran' August 1913. On file at ACHS.
-McCreary, Alburtus. Gettysburg, A Boys Experience of the Battle. McClure's Magazine Vol. XXXIII, May to Oct. 1909. Copy at ACHS.
-Sloan, I. O. The German Reformed Messenger, Chambersburg, Pa. July 28, 1863. On file ACHS.
-Tipton, William. Presentation of the Memorial Tablet Commemorating the Lincoln-Burns

Event, Nov. 19, 1914. Pamphlet containing Tiptons speech on his recollection of that event. On file ACHS.

-Trowbridge, J. T. The Field of Gettysburg, Atlantic Monthly, Nov. 16, 1865. Copy of text on file at ACHS.

-Warren, Mary (Fasnacht). Memories of the Battle of Gettysburg, The Princely Press. NY, NY. 1941. On file at the ACHS.

Unpublished Manuscripts:

-Barr, Agnes. Account of the Battle of Gettysburg (no date). On file ACHS.

-Buehler, Fannie. Recollections of the Great Rebel Invasion and One Woman's Experience During the Battle of Gettysburg. On file ACHS.

-Fahnestock, Gates D. Test of speech given before the National Arts Club of New York, Feb. 12, 1934. On file ACHS.

-Georg, Kathleen R. (Harrison). "This Grand National Enterprise": The Origins of Gettysburg's Soldiers National Cemetery and the Gettysburg Battlefield Memorial Association. 1982. On file GNMP.

-Jacobs, Henry E. How an Eye Witness Watched the Great Battle. On file ACHS.

-Monfort, Mary Elizabeth. How a 12 Year Old Girl Saw Gettysburg. Copy of text published in the Doylestown, Pa. Daily Register May 30, 1959. On file ACHS.

-Patriot Daughters of Lancaster. Hospital Scenes After The Battle of Gettysburg. Lancaster, Pa. 1863. Reprinted by G. Craig Caba. 1993.

-Warren, Leander. What I Saw Before, During and After the Battle of Gettysburg. Copy on file at ACHS.

-Will, John C. Reminiscences of The Three Days Battle of Gettysburg. Copy on file at the ACHS.

-Ziegler, Catherine (Clare). A Gettysburg Girl's Story of the Great Battle 1900. On file ACHS.

Newspapers:

-The Adams Sentinel*
-The Gettysburg Compiler*
-Phila. Evening Bulletin**
-Phila. Inquirer**
-Doylestown Daily Register**
-The Star and Banner*
-Globe-Democrat Brookfield Mo.**
-Phila. North American**
-Phila. Weekly Press**

*On microfilm at ACHS.   **Copy of referenced article(s) on file at ACHS.

Letters:

-McCreary, Jennie. Letter to her sister Julia, July 22, 1863. Copy on file at ACHS.

-Rupp, John. Letter to his sister, July 19, 1863. Copy on file at ACHS.

-Sweney, Harvey. Letter to his brother Andrew, Nov. 29, 1963. Courtesy of Loren Schultz.

END NOTES

INTRODUCTION

1. Jennie S. Croll, "Days of Dread": A Woman's Story of Her Life on the Battlefield. A narrative published in the PHILADELPHIA WEEKLY PRESS, Nov. 16, 1887. Copy on file at the Adams County Historical Society, hereafter cited as ACHS. Jennie Croll, the wife of Professor Luther H. Croll, was not a citizen of Gettysburg in 1863 and did not experience first hand the events described in this memoir. Evidence points to Mary Horner, wife of Dr. Robert Horner, as the first person in the narrative. While admittedly speculative, it is the authors conclusion that the person who lived these experiences is Mary Horner, and they are attributed to her in this narrative. Hereafter cited as, Jennie Croll; "Days of Dread".

2. ADAMS SENTINEL, July 7, 1863.

3. 1860 U.S. Census for the Borough of Gettysburg, Adams County, Pa.

4. John W. Busey and David G. Martin, Regimental Strengths and Losses at Gettysburg. Published by Longstreet House, Hightstown, N.J. 1986. All reference to manpower numbers of both armies throughout this document are cited from Busey and Martin.

5. Robert L. Bloom, A History of Adams County Pennsylvania 1700-1990. Published by the Adams County Historical, Gettysburg, Pa. 1992. p 179

6. John C. Will, Reminiscences of The Three Days Battle of Gettysburg at the Globe Hotel. An unpublished manuscript on file at the ACHS. Hereafter cited as John Will, Reminiscences..

JUNE 15th-30th: "Unmistakeable signs..began to accumulate"

1. GETTYSBURG COMPILER, June 24, 1908.

2. Ibid.

3. Ibid.

4. Charles M. McCurdy, Gettysburg: A Memoir. Published by the Reed and Witting Co., Pittsburg, Pa. 1929. p 9. Hereafter cited as Charles McCurdy.

5. Ibid, p 10

6. Leander Warren, What I Saw Before, During and After The Battle of Gettysburg. An unpublished manuscript on file at the ACHS. Hereafter cited as Warren, What I Saw..

7. 1860 U.S. Census.

8. Tillie Pierce Alleman, At Gettysburg, or What a Young Girl Saw and Heard of the Battle. Published by W. Lake Borland, New York, NY. 1889. p 18. Hereafter cited as Tillie Pierce Alleman.

9. John Wills, Reminiscences..

10. THE COMPILER, October 20, 1862. On microfilm at ACHS.

11. Jennie McCreary, Letter to Her Sister Julia, July 22, 1863. Reprinted in the PHILADELPHIA EVENING BULLETIN, July 2, 1938. A copy on file at ACHS. Hereafter cited as Jennie McCreary, Letter to Julia..

12. Michael Jacobs, The Rebel Invasion of Maryland and Pennsylvania and the Battle of Gettysburg. Published by J. B. Lippincott and Co. Philadelphia, Pa., 1864. p 6. Hereafter cited as Michael Jacobs.

13. Sarah Broadhead, A Diary of a Lady of Gettysburg. Privately printed. A copy on hand at ACHS. Daily entries of events from June 15th through July 14th. Hereafter cited as Sarah Broadhead, A Diary of a Lady.

14. Fannie Buehler, Recollections of the Great Rebel Invasion and One Woman's Experiences During the Battle of Gettysburg. Written in 1896. A copy on file at ACHS. Hereafter cited as Fannie Buehler, Recollections..

15. Salome Myers Stewart, Recollections of the Battle of Gettysburg, an interview published in the PHILADELPHIA NORTH AMERICAN, July 7, 1900. Hereafter cited as Salome Myers Stewart, Recollections..

16. Sarah Broadhead, A Diary of a Lady: Fannie Buehler, Recollections. There is a descrepancey between Broadhead and Buehler as to what night this incident took place. Sarah Broadhead recorded it in her entry for June 16th. Fannie Buhler, writing 34 years after the event said it was, "June 20th, I think." I have followed Sarah's contemporary version.

17. Salome Myers Stewart, Recollection . . Dairy entry for June 17th.

18. Fannie Buehler, Recollections..

19. Samuel G. Hefelbower. History of Gettysburg College 1832-1932. p. 184.

20. Michael Jacobs, p 9

21. Sarah Broadhead, A Diary of a Lady. Entry for June 24th.

22. Ibid

23. Ibid

24. ADAMS SENTINEL, July 7, 1863. Copy on microfilm at ACHS. The troops of the 26th Pa. Emer Vol. were totally without military experience. They had received virtually no small unit drill or rifle practice in the few days that they were in Camp Curtin in Harrisburg. They were certainly not fit to face the likes of veteran Confederate infantry. That so few were hurt in their clash with the Rebels is one of the battle's many small miracles.

25. Henry Eyster Jacobs, How an Eye Witness Watched the Great Battle. Copy of the manuscript on file at ACHS. Hereafter cited as Henry E. Jacobs, How an Eye Witness..

26. Mary Elizabeth Montfort, How a 12 Year Old Girl Saw Gettysburg. Reminiscences published in the DAILY REGISTER, Doylestown, Pa. May 30, 1959. A transcript of the article is on file at ACHS. Hereafter cited as Mary Elizabeth Montfort, How a 12 Year Old Girl..: Mary Warren Fastnacht, Memories of the Battle of Gettysburg. The Princely Press, NY, NY, 1941. Copy on file at ACHS. Hereafter cited as Mary Warren Fastnacht, Memories..

27. Sarah Broadhead, A Diary of a Lady. June 26th entry.

28. Tillie Pierce Alleman. p 21

29. Sue Myers, "Some Battle Experiences as Remembered by a Young School Girl." GETTYSBURG COMPILER, April 24, 1907. On microfilm at ACHS. Sue Myers was the younger sister of Salome Myers.

30. Tillie Pierce Alleman. p 21

31. John Will, Battle Days at the Globe Inn. GETTYSBURG COMPILER, July 7, 1910. Will identified Jim Furley, a former resident of Gettysburg and a Confederate accomplice, as the one who told Harvey Wattles about the disappointment in not getting the telegraph apparatus. The two men met in the bar at the Globe Inn and Will overheard their conversation. Will quotes Furley as saying: "I wish I could have gotten your telegraph apparatus. I would have fooled your men, but it was gone." Jim Furley was the same man Sarah King claimed had attempted to rob his old employer, the blacksmith, Adam Doersom.

32. Fannie Buehler, Recollections..

33. Charles McCurdy, pp 10-11

34. Sarah Broadhead, A Diary of a Lady: Charles McCurdy, p 11: Gates D. Fahnestock, Speech Given Before the National Arts Club of New York, February 12, 1934. Copy of the text on file at ACHS. Hereafter cited as Gates Fahnestock, Speech..

35. Tillie Pierce Alleman, p 22: John Wills, Reminiscences..

36. Tillie Pierce Alleman, pp 24-27. Cindy L. Small, in her book (The Jennie Wade Story, Thomas Publications, Gettysburg, Pa. 1991 pp 19-20. Hereafter cited as Cindy L. Small, The Jennie Wade Story) gives an entirely different version of this incident. In Ms. Small's narrative, Jennie Wade was the one who first negotiated with Sam's captors for his release. When she was unsuccessful, Jennie proceeded to her sisters house and informed her mother of the crisis. Her mother, Mary Wade, then went directly to General Early and secured the release of young Sam, who then returned to the Pierce house to wait out the departure of the enemy. No mention is made of any involvement on the part of the Pierces

in helping to get Sam away from the Confederates. The two versions do agree on the fact that the Pierces did not get their horse back.

There is a new piece of information just acquired (1994) by the ACHS that sheds some confirming light on the Tillie Pierce Alleman version. This is an undated, unsigned, hand written statement by a eye witness to the event. The theme of the letter is that Jennie named Pierce as a "Black Abolishonist" and for some reason was out of sorts with the Pierce's for Sam's predicament.

As usual the truth undoubtedly encompasses some elements of both versions. The author has made a judgement decision to present the Tillie Alleman version as the one representing the facts in this matter.

37. Sarah King, A Mother's Story. The GETTYSBURG COMPILER, July 4, 1906. Hereafter cited as Sarah King, A Mother's Story.

38. Leander Warren, What I Saw..: Fannie Buehler, Recollections.. Fannie claimed: "I find I have thought more (about the burning) of the courthouse than I did of my own house."

39. John Will, Reminiscences..

40. Margaretta Kendlehart McCartney, A Story of Early's Raid. GETTYSBURG COMPILER, June 30, 1923.

41. Michael Jacobs, p 16: Sarah Barrett King, A Mother's Story: Albertus McCreary, Gettysburg, A Boy's Experience of the Battle. McClure's Magazine, July, 1909. A copy of the typescript of this article is on file at ACHS. Hereafter cited as Albertus McCreary, A Boy's Experience..

42. Charles McCurdy, p 13

43. John Will, Reminiscences..

44. Albertus McCreary, A Boy's Experience...: Blacks were not the only citizens at risk. When the Rebel Army retreated on July 5th, they took with them eight white citizens from the Gettysburg area as captives. These men were not released from prison in Salisbury, N.C. until the Spring of 1865.

45. Mary Warren Fastnatch, Memories..

46. Sarah King, A Mother's Story..: Albertus McCreary, A Boy's Experience..

47. Daniel Skelly, A Boy's Experiences During the Battle of Gettysburg. Privately Printed, Gettysburg, Pa. 1932. Hereafter cited as Daniel Skelly. A copy is on file at ACHS.

48. Fannie Buehler, Recollections..

49. Michael Jacobs, p 16: Henry Eyster Jacobs, How An Eye Witness..

50. Michael Jacobs, p 19.

51. Alice Powers, Dark Days of the Battle Week. GETTYSBURG COMPILER, July 1, 1903. Copy on microfilm at ACHS. Hereafter cited as Alice Powers, Dark Days..

52. Agnes Barr, Account of the Battle of Gettysburg. Unpublished manuscript (n.d.) on file at the ACHS. Hereafter cited as Agnes Barr, Account of the Battle..

53. Catherine Foster, The Story of the Battle, An account published in the GETTYSBURG COMPILIER, June 6, 1904. Hereafter cited as Catherine Foster, The Story of the Battle.

54. Salome Myers, Dairy Entry, June 28th.

55. Catherine Foster, The story of the Battle.

56. Daniel Skelly, p 10

57. Catherine Foster, The Story of the Battle.

58. Alice Powers, Dark Days..

59. Sarah Broadhead, A Diary of a Lady. June 30th entry: Michael Jacobs, p 21

60. Catherine Foster, The Story of the Battle.

61. George W. Martin, Brookfield, Mo. GLOBE-DEMOCRAT. July 1, 1903. Copy on file at ACHS.

62. Alice Powers, Dark Days: Salome Myers Stewart, Recollections: Tillie Pierce, p 29. The girls that gathered along S. Washington Street on June 30th to serenade the troopers were: Anna Garlach, Livinia C. Weirick, Carrie Young, Mary A. Culp, Amanda Reinecker, Sallie McClellan, Sue Myers, Salome Myers and Dorothy Fleming.

63. Gates Fahnestock, Speech..: Charles McCurdy, p 15

64. W.C. Hazelton, Interview published by the STAR AND SENTINEL, September 1,1891. On microfilm at ACHS.

65. Anna Garlach Kitzmiller, Mrs Kitzmiller's Story, published in the GETTYSBURG COMPILER, August 9 & 23, 1905. Hereafter cited as Anna Garlach Kitzmiller, Her Story.

66. John Will, Reminiscences..

67. Catherine Foster, The Story of the Battle: Charles McCurdy, p 15: Daniel Skelly, p 10: Tillie Pierce Alleman, p 30: Albertus McCreary, A Boy's Experience..

68. Fannie Buehler, Recollections..

JULY 1ST: "...an awful reality"

1. Lydia Catherine Ziegler Clare, A Gettysburg Girl's Story of the Great Battle. Unpublished account on file at ACHS. Hereafter cited as Catherine Ziegler Clare, A Gettysburg Girl's Story...

2. Henry Eyster Jacobs, How an Eye Witness..: Sarah Broadhead, A Diary of a Lady: Charles Tyson, his account published in the PHILADELPHIA WEEKLY, March 29, 1884. Copy on file at ACHS. Hereafter cited as Charles Tyson, Account.

3. Lydia Ziegler Clare, A Gettysburg Girl's Story..

4. Leander Warren, What I Saw..

5. Jennie S. Croll, "Days of Dread".

6. Sarah King, A Mother's Story.

7. Tillie Pierce Alleman, p 33: Anna Garlach Kitzmiller, Her Story.

8. Sarah Broadhead, A Diary of a Lady.

9. Salome Myers Stewart, Recollections..

10. Daniel Skelly, p 11

11. Charles McCurdy, pp 15,16

12. William McClean, Days of Terror in 1863. Article published in the GETTYSBURG COMPILER, June 1, 1908. Hereafter cited as William McClean, Days of Terror..

13. Catherine Ziegler Clare, A Gettysburg Girl's Story..

14. Gates Fahnestock, Speech..: Nellie Aughinbaugh, Personal Experiences of a Young Girl During the Battle of Gettysburg. Privately printed, 1941. p 6. Copy on file at ACHS. Hereafter cited as Nellie Aughinbaugh, Personal Experiences..: Robert McClean, A Boy in Gettysburg, GETTYSBURG COMPILER, June 30, 1909. Copy on microfilm at ACHS. Hereafter cited as Robert McClean, A Boy in Gettysburg: Elizabeth McClean, "The Rebels Are Coming," GETTYSBURG COMPILER, July 8, 1908. Copy on microfilm at ACHS. Hereafter cited as Elizabeth McClean, "The Rebels Are Coming."

15. Daniel Skelly, pp 12-14

16. Catherine Foster, The Story of the Battle.

17. Charles Tyson, Account..

18. General Lee's Headquarters Museum. The china set along with an account of Mrs. Felty's purchase, and the china's survival of a near miss by an artillery shell was on display in the museum. Now(2008) in a private collection.

19. John Will, Reminiscences..

20. Salome Myers Stewart, Recollections..

21. Mary McAllister, An Interview published (posthumously) in the PHILADELPHIA INQUIRER, June 26-29, 1938. Hereafter cited as Mary McAllister, An Interview.

22. Ibid

23. Mary Elizabeth Montfort, How a 12 Year Old Girl..

24. Charles Tyson, Account.

25. Charles McCurdy, p 17. Charles' grandmother, Ann McCurdy, was a "..stately 90 years old." Because of her age she probably had someone living with her to help with the house upkeep and to look after her safety. Based on Agnes Barr's (her next door neighbor) account it is believed a Mrs. White and her two daughters were living there at the time.

26. Jennie S. Croll, "Days of Dread"

27. Mrs. Jacob (Liberty Hollinger) Glutz, Some Personal Recollections of the Battle of Gettysburg. Privately printed, 1925. pp 2,3. Copy on file at ACHS. Hereafter cited as Liberty Hollinger Glutz, Personal Recollections.. The two officers were Lts. Loyd B. Harris and John Beely of the 6th Wisconsin. Harris left a detail account of their visit to the Hollinger house which is quoted in, IN THE BLOODY RAIL ROAD CUT AT GETTYSBURG, by Lance J. Herdegen and William J. K. Beaudot. Morningside House, Inc., Dayton, Ohio. 1990. pp 221-223. There are some interesting discrepancies in the comparison of Harris' and Liberty Hollinger's accounts of the visit by the officers. Harris claims that he and Beely were also accompanied by Lt. William Remington who was shot in the shoulder as he tried to seize the colors of the 2nd Missisippi. Liberty Hollinger does not mention the presence of Lt. Remington. One would imagine that a shoulder gunshot wound would have been sufficient to keep a person from walking about the town. Harris had a buckshot removed from the fleshy part of his neck. Beely had a wrist wound. All the wounds had been attended to before they came upon the Hollingers, according to Harris. Harris mentions a "..hasty meal.." taken with the Hollingers. Liberty says they were dealing with the decision to leave or stay and makes no mention of a meal. Harris claimed that he found Sgt. William Evans of the 6th Wisc. upstairs in a bed with serious leg wounds. He further claims that Evans had been entrusted with the captured flag belonging to the 2nd Miss. when he hobbled from the field (Why one so wounded in the legs would have walked all the way through town, past several hospitals before finding a private home in which to have his wounds dressed is difficult to fathom). When it was time to move on as the 11th Corp fled the field, Evans had to be left with the Hollingers. Harris describes in detail how the bed ticking Evans was lying upon was cut by Liberty and her sister Julia and the flag inserted to avoid detection should the Confederates come searching. At last Harris recalls urging the family to the cellar, almost as an after thought, as he was leaving. Liberty makes no mention of a Sgt. Evans or hiding a captured flag but does credit Harris with urging them to go to the cellar and helping to transport her invalid mother. Harris' story made good copy for the veterans, some 17 years later. I suspect Liberty's account comes closer to history.

28. Jennie S. Croll, "Days of Dread."

29. William Tipton. Presentation of the Memorial Tablet Commemorating the Lincoln Burns Event. Nov. 19, 1914.

30. Mary McAllister, An Interview.

31. Albertus McCreary, A Boy's Experience..

32. Catherine Foster, The Story of the Battle: Alice Powers, Dark Days..

33. Leander Warren, What I Saw..

34. Daniel Skelly, p 15

35. Robert McClean, A Boy in Gettysburg: Elizabeth McClean, "The Rebels Are Coming."

36. Henry Eyster Jacobs, How an Eye Witness..

37. Mary McAllister, An Interview.

38. Ibid

39. Jennie S. Croll, "Days of Dread."

40. Salome Myers Stewart, Recollections..

41. Catherine Foster, The Story of the Battle.

42. Charles McCurdy, p 18

43. Albertus McCreary, A Boy's Experience

44. Anna Garlach Kitzmiller, Her Story..

45. Sarah Broadhead, A Diary of a Lady.

46. Henry Eyster Jacobs, How an Eye Witness..

47. Catherine Foster, The Story of the Battle.

48. Salome Myers Stewart, Recollections..: Alice Powers, Dark Days..

49. Albertus McCreary, A Boy's Experience..

50. William McClean, Days of Terror..

51. Daniel Skelly, pp 15,16

52. Frank Moore. Women of the War. S. S. Scranton & Co. Hartford Conn. 1866. p 242.

53. Liberty Hollinger Glutz, Personal Recollections.. p 3

54. Albertus McCreary, A Boy's Experience..

55. Fannie Buehler, Recollections..: Sue Elizabeth Stoever, A Woman's Story of the Town. GETTYSBURG COMPILER, June 24, 1909. Copy on microfilm at ACHS. Hereafter cited as Elizabeth Stoever, A Woman's Story..

56. Elizabeth Gilbert, an interview published in the GETTYSBURG COMPLIER, September 6, 1905. Copy on microfilm at ACHS. Hereafter cited as Elizabeth Gilbert, An Interview.

57. Fannie Buehler, Recollections . .

58. Charles McCurdy, p 19

59. Anna Garlach Kitzmiller, Her Story . .

60. Catherine Foster, The Story of the Battle.

61. Alice Powers, Dark Days..

62. Sarah Broadhead, A Diary of a Lady.

63. John Will, Reminiscences..

64. Jennie McCreary, Letter to Julia..

65. J. Howard Wert, Little Stories of Gettysburg. GETTYSBURG COMPILER,

January 1, 1908. On microfilm at ACHS.

66. Elizabeth Thorn, GETTYSBURG COMPILER, July 26, 1905.

67. Leander Warren, What I Saw: William McClean, Days of Terror..

68. Salome Myers Stewart, Recollections..

69. Agnes Barr, Account of the Battle..: Gates Fahnestock, Speech..

70. Charles McCurdy, p 22.

71. Alice Powers, Dark Days.

JULY 2ND: "O! how I dread tomorrow"

1. Sarah Broadhead, A Diary of a Lady. If Sarah literally referred to the house standing directly across the street it would have been the home of William Boyer (#214 Chambersburg St.). Boyer and his family, in the company of his next door neighbors Charles and Maria Tyson, left Gettysburg for Littlestown, ten miles away, in the early afternoon of July 1st.

2. Mary McAllister, An Interview..

3. Catherine Foster, The Story of the Battle.

4. Elizabeth McClean, "The Rebels Are Coming".

5. Daniel Skelly, p 16

6. Henry Eyster Jacobs, How an Eye Witness..: Mary Warren Fastnatch, Memoirs..: Leander Warren, What I Saw..: Daniel Skelly, p 19

7. Leander Warren, What I Saw..

8. John Will, Reminiscences..

9. Robert McClean, A Boy in Gettysburg..: Charles McCurdy, p 22: Fannie Buehler, Recollections..: Jennie S. Croll, "Days of Dread."

10. William McClean, Days of Terror..

11. Mary McAllister, An Interview

12. Elizabeth McClean, "The Rebels Are Coming."

13. John Will, Reminiscences..

14. Nellie Aughinbaugh, Personal Experiences.. p 9: Gates Fahnestock, Speech..: Fannie Buehler, Recollections..

15. Nellie Aughinbaugh, Personal Experiences . . p 8: Liberty Hollinger Glutz, Personal Recollectons.. p 4. Liberty descibes the "havoc" left in the warehouse by the Confederates. For some reason they turned on the molasses barrel spigots and left them to drain all over the floor. They wantonly scattered salt and sugar (valuable commodities to the Confederates) on the floor as well: "Poor father was quite ill because of the havoc they wrought in his place of business."

16. Mary Elizabeth Montfort, How a 12 Year old Girl..

17. Alice Powers, Dark Days: J. Howard Wert, "Little Stories of Gettysburg." The GETTYSBURG COMPILER, January 8, 1908. Hereafter cited as J. Howard Wert, "Little Stories of Gettysburg."

18. Mary McAllister, An Interview

19. Charles McCurdy, p 20: Alice Powers, Dark Days.

20. Daniel Skelly, p 17

21. John Rupp, A letter to his sister Anne, July 19, 1863. Copy of this letter on file at ACHS.

22. Anna Garlach Kitzmiller, Her Story.. The families seeking shelter in the Garlach cellar were Hannah Bream and daughter, the Sullivan family, and the McIlroy family.

23. Ibid

24. Ibid

25. Ibid. The scar made by the bullet in the garret window jamb is still present today. It is not readily visible from the outside due to being covered by the aluminum siding presently on all external wood work.

26. M.L. Culler, "Interesting Incidents Connected With the Battle of Gettysburg." GETTYSBURG COMPILER, July 19, 1911.

27. Gettysburg National Military Park Visitors Center Museum. The table from the Samuel McCreary house is on display with a label that gives the details of Poole's use and death, which actually took place on July 3rd.

28. Albertus McCreary, A Boy's Experience..

29. William McClean, Days of Terror.. The bed with the bullet hole in the footboard and the bullet recovered by McClean from the mattress are on display at the GNMP Visitors Center Museum.

30. Salome Myers Stewart, Recollections..

31. Liberty Hollinger Glutz, Personal Recollections.. p 5,6

32. John Will, Reminiscences

33. Henry Eyster Jacobs, How an Eye Witness..

34. Daniel Skelly, p 17

35. Gregory A. Coco, War Stories: A Collection of 150 Little Known Human Interest Accounts of the Campaign and Battle of Gettysburg.

36. Tillie Pierce Alleman, pp 96,97. Tillie, who was not present in Gettysburg to witness this event, includes it in her memoirs and fixes the date as July 1st. In this author's opinion, there is good reason to suspect that she is mistaken about the date on which it occurred. The majority of incidents of shells striking buildings in Gettysburg were reported as happening during the artillery exchanges that sent shells over the town on July 2nd and 3rd. It appears more likely that the event of the shell striking the Bergstresser house happened on one of those two days. I have made the assumption that it occurred on July 2nd.

37. Mary McAllister, An Interview.

38. Sarah Broadhead, A Diary of a Lady: Elizabeth Gilbert, An Interview. In her account that was given to the GETTYSBURG COMPILER 42 years after the event, Mrs. Gilbert places the date as July 3rd. Sarah Broadhead wrote in her diary that it happened on July 2nd. Sarah's account is probably accurate since her diary entries were contemporary with the events as they occurred.

39. Michael Sellinger. Affidavit given Sept. 9, 1916. Copy on file ACHS.

40. Henry Eyster Jacobs, How an Eye Witness..: Albertus McCreary, A Boy's Experience..:Fannie Buehler, Recollectons..

41. Agnes Barr, Account of the Battle..

42. Mary McAllister, An Interview..

43. Ibid

44. Gates Fahnestock, Speech..: William McClean, Days of Terror..: Catherine Foster, The Story of the Battle.

45. Elizabeth McClean, "The Rebels Are Coming"

JULY 3RD: "..it seemed as if the Heavens and Earth were crashing together"

1. Sarah Broadhead, A Diary of Lady.

2. Catherine Foster, The Story of the Battle. Catherine found a certain irony in the destruction brought about by the shell that penetrated the bedroom: "It is said of George Washington that no bullet had been made to penetrate his body..A picture of Washington (crossing the Delaware River) stood beneath the mantle of the room in which the two Doctors slept. The shell, which entered through the jamb of the fire place sending the mantle across the room, broke the frame and glass to "smithereens," but the picture remained unscathed."

3. Elizabeth McClean, "The Rebels Are Coming." The artillery shells that were so terrorizing to the citizens whose houses were struck, strangely became a badge of honor following the battle. Many home owners placed a shell in the wall where they struck to signify to tourist and fellow townspeople that they had been hit during the battle. A few are still visible today and are pointed out by guides as buildings with the distinction of having been "wounded" during the battle.

4. Cindy L. Small, The Jennie Wade Story. p 34

5. J.T. Trowbridge, The Field of Gettysburg. The Atlantic Monthly, November 16, 1865. An interview with John Burns. At the time of the interview (1865) Burn's house was still standing and Trowbridge visited the site and saw the bullet holes in the wall and door.

Trowbridge, in his article, offered some interesting observations on Burn's status in the community and on his personality: "Burns became a hero..however there are a lot of dissenters in the town with his hero status." Trowbridge claims: "..the young men who choose not to follow his example and take up arms and fight, dislike Burns." Trowbridge acknowledged that Burns was ,"..a zealous Patriot..," given to "..immoderate opinions..," and prone to making "..immoderate statements..." Burns was particularly harsh in his post battle comments concerning Jennie Wade's character. It must be remembered that Burn's was forced to share fame at Gettysburg with Jennie, which just might have colored his opinion about her.

6. Elizabeth McClean, "The Rebels Are Coming."

7. Liberty Hollinger Glutz, Personal Recollections.. pp 4 & 15

8. John Will, Reminiscences..

9. Nellie Aughinbaugh, Personal Experiences.. pp 9,10

10. Albertus McCreary, A Boy's Experience..

11. Ibid

12. Robert McClean, A Boy in Gettysburg..

13. Salome Myers Stewart, Recollections..

14. Agnes Barr, Account of the Battle..

15. Sarah Broadhead, A Diary of a Lady.

16. Henry Eyster Jacobs, How an Eye Witness..

17. Albertus McCreary, A Boy's Experience..: Jennie McCreary, A Letter to Julia..

18. Henry Eyster Jacobs, How an Eye Witness..

19. Charles McCurdy, p 23: Albertus McCreary, A Boy's Experience..

20. Agnes Barr, Account of the Battle..

21. William McClean, Days of Terror..

22. Mary McAllister, An Interview.

23. Anna Garlach Kitzmiller, Her Story.

24. Sarah Broadhead, A Diary of a Lady: Catherine Foster, The Story of the Battle.

25. John Will, Reminiscences..

26. Ibid

27. Elizabeth McClean, "Here Come the Rebels."

28. Elizabeth Stoever, A Woman's Story..

JULY 4TH: "..resurrected from an untold ordeal"

1. Mary McAllister, An Interview..

2. Elizabeth McClean, "The Rebels Are Coming:" Agnes Barr, Account of the Battle..

3. Henry Monath, Unwritten History, A Narrative. Published in the GETTYSBURG COMPILER, December 28, 1897. Copy on microfilm at ACHS.

4. Jennie McCreary, A Letter to Julia..

5. Daniel Skelly, p 19: Catherine Foster, The Story of the Battle: Sarah Broadhead, A Diary of a Lady: Mary McAllister, An Interview.

6. Alice Powers, Dark Days.

7. John Will, Reminiscences..

8. Mary McAllister, An Interview.

9. Tillie Pierce Alleman, p 99,100: Robert McClean, A Boy in Gettysburg.

10. Albertus McCreary, A Boy's Experience..: Catherine Foster, The Story of the Battle: Anna Garlach Kitzmiller, Her Story.

11. Henry Eyster Jacobs, How an Eye Witness..

12. Mary Warren Fastnatch, Memoirs..

13. Ibid

14. Gates Fahnestock, Speech..

15. Elizabeth Stoever, A Woman's Story.. Mrs Stoever made no mention as to where she and the children went to stay outside of Gettysburg for "a few days."

16. Robert McClean, A Boy in Gettysburg.

17. Elizabeth Gilbert, An Interview.

18. Mary McAllister, An Interview: The two other citizens allegedly wounded according to the ADAMS SENTINEL, were a Mr. Lehman and R. F. McIlhenny, both in the leg.

19. Jennie S. Croll, "Days of Dread."

20. William McClean, Days of Terror..

21. Agnes Barr, Account of the Battle: John L. Schick, Recollections printed in the PHILADELPHIA NORTH AMERICAN, July 4, 1909.

22. Alice Powers, Dark Days..

23. Sarah Broadhead, A Diary of a Lady.

JULY 5TH - AUGUST 1ST: "..the people of Gettysburg assisted in everyway"

1. Albertus McCreary, A Boy's Experience..: Nellie Aughinbaugh, Personal Experiences.. p 10

2. William McClean, Days of Terror..

3. Nellie Aughinbaugh, Personal Experiences.. pp 10,11

4. John Will, Reminiscences.. While the Confederates were in possession of the town, John harbored some curiosity as to why they did not patronize the other hotels as they did the Globe. At one point he asked an officer:"Why do you Confederates all gather up here (the Globe Inn)?" The reply: "The Army of Northern Virginia knew of the Globe Inn long before they came into Pa." The Wills' were staunch Democrats. The other establishments in town were owned by Republicans. The Confederates would naturally be inclined not to trust the latter anti-slavery proponents to provide them with food and drink.

5. Henry Stahle editorial in THE COMPILER, October 9, 1865.

6. Charles McCurdy, p 27

7. Gregory A. Coco, On the Bloodstained Field II. Thomas Publications, Gettysburg, Pa. 1989. p 84

8. Mary McAllister, An Interview. Several days after Mary gave the Gen'l. Archer sword to Col. Morrow, probably on July 7th, Lt. Dennis Baily showed up at the Scott house seeking his prized trophy. When Mary heard the familiar voice explaining to her sister , "I have come back for the sword," her heart fell. She could do nothing but explain what happened, assuring Baily that she thought, "..he was in Libby Prison." Baily had effected his escape while on route back towards the Potomac River. He was disappointed, but understanding. A few months later he wrote Mary that he had come across Col. Morrow and reclaimed his sword. After the war he presented it to his old brigade commander, Col. Solomon Meredith. When Meredith died in 1875, it passed to the Iron Brigade Association and once again Dennis Baily sought to reclaim it. He appealed to Mary to write a letter supporting his claim of having it in his possession on July 1st, 1863. Mary complied with his request and a short while later General Archer's Gettysburg sword was reunited with Lt. Baily. Today it is in the hands of an unidentified, private collector.

9. Fannie Buehler, Recollections..

10. William McClean, Days of Terror..: Salome Myers Stewart, Recollections..: J. Howard Wert, "Little Stories of Gettysburg"

11. Sarah Broadhead, A Diary of a Lady.

12. Catherine Ziegler Clare, A Gettysburg Girl's Story..

13. Elizabeth Thorn, GETTYSBURG COMPILER, July 26, 1905.

14. Charles Tyson, Account of the Battle..: Sarah Broadhead, A Diary of a Lady: Liberty Hollinger Glutz, Some Personal Recollections..

15. Albertus McCreary, A Boy's Experience..

16. Agnes Barr, Account of the Battle..

17. Fannie Buehler, Recollections..

18. Albertus McCreary, A Boy's Experience..

19. Elizabeth Stoever, A Woman's Story.. When Elizabeth and her children returned to town on the 7th, she found: "..the guest chamber occupied by two women devoting their days to nursing...Dr. Stoever's generosity and connections with the Christian Commission opened the doors to those engaged in ministering the wounded." Her observations of the town scene leave us with an insight as to the mix of chaos and joy in the first days following the Confederate withdrawal: "There were sad sights throughout the town..public buildings and private homes filled with suffering (wounded); embalmers and commissary departments occupying the stores of the merchants. Pathetic and humorous were the meetings of friends and relatives who, having been separated by the strange adventures of war, laughed and cried as they recounted their experiences."

20. Cornelia Hancock, The South After Gettysburg: Letters of Cornelia Hancock. Ed. Henrietta S. Jaquette, University of Pennsylvania Press, Philadelphia, Pa. 1937. p 71

21. Ibid, p 100

22. Like Angel's Wings, The Sister of Charity. Battlefield Journal 1999.

23. The Patriot Daughters of Lancaster. Hospital Scenes . . . pp.24-46. Hereafter cited as Patriot Daughters.

24. John Wills, Reminiscences..

25. Gates Fahnestock, Speech.. According to Gates, "..some 12 or 13," Union soldiers came into his house seeking shelter during the confusion of the retreat on July 1st. "Confederates came looking for them..and found everyone but one, a Ohio captain (McDaniel). He later gave himself up.:" Elizabeth McClean, "The Rebels Are Coming;" Liberty Hollinger Glutz, Personal Recollections.. pp 14,15

26. Leander Warren, What I Saw..

27. John Wills, Reminiscences..

28. Albertus McCreary, A Boy's Experience..: Charles McCurdy, p 28

29. Nellie Aughinbaugh, Personal Experiences.. p 13

30. Ibid, p 14

31. John Rupp, Letter to his sister, Anne, July 19, 1863.

32. Patriot Daughters. p. 28.

33. Catherine Foster, The Story of the Battle..

34. Fannie Buehler, Recollections..

35. Anna Garlach Kitzmiller, Her Story..

36. Tillie Pierce Alleman, pp 101-103

37. Gregory A. Coco, A Vast Sea of Misery. Thomas Publications, Gettysburg, Pa. 1988. p 47

38. Sarah Broadhead, A Diary of a Lady.

39. Ibid

40. Ibid

41. L.O. Sloan, Narrative published in the GERMAN REFORMED MESSENGER, July 7, 1913. Copy on file at ACHS.

42. Jennie McCreary, Letter to Julia..

43. Daniel Skelly, p 25

44. Gates Fahnestock, Speech..

<u>AFTERWARD:</u> "The world will little note nor long remember.."

1. Henry Eyster Jacobs,How An Eye Witness..

2. ADAMS SENTINEL, August 19, 1863.

3. David McConaughy, Letter to Andrew Curtin, July 25, 1863. Quoted in Kathleen R. Georg (Harrison), "This Grand National Enterprise":The Origins of Gettysburg's Soldiers' National Cemetery and the Gettysburg Battlefield Memorial Association. Gettysburg National Military Park (GNMP), May and November 1982. Unpublished manuscript. p 16.

4. Harlan D. Unrau, Administrative History, Gettysburg National Military Park and National Cemetery. U.S. Department of the Interior, 1991. pp 8,9

5. David Wills, Letter to Andrew Curtin, July 24, 1863. Quoted in Kathleen Georg, "This Grand National Enterprise". p 10

6. Theodore S. Dimon, Letter to John F. Seymour, August 1, 1863. Quoted in Kathleen Georg, "This Grand National Enterprise." Kathy Georg Harrison, Chief Historian at the GNMP, explores the issue of who really initiated the concept of a Soldier's National Cemetery, and as such, who should be correctly labeled as the "father." As always, her research is thorough, and her analysis presents a compelling case to support Dr. Theodore Dimon's claim to the title. Her manuscript, "This Grand National Enterprise," should be published.

7. Harvey Sweney, Letter to his brother Andrew dated November 29, 1863.

8. Garry Wills, Lincoln At Gettysburg. Simon and Schuster, NY, NY. 1992. p 30. Hereafter cited as Garry Wills: Daniel Skelly, p 26

9. D. Mark Katz, article printed in the GETTYSBURG TIMES, December 14, 1985.

10. Daniel Skelly, p 25

11. Liberty Hollinger Glutz, Personal Recollections.. pp 19-22

12. Harvey Sweney, Letter..

13. Daniel Skelly, p 27: Rev. H.C. Holloway, D.D., Lincoln at Gettysburg, Recollections of H.C. Holloway, D.D.. The GETTYSBURG COMPILER, November 21, 1913. Hereafter cited as H.C. Holloway, Lincoln at Gettysburg..

14. Garry Wills, pp 205-210. The actual location of the site of the 12'x20' platform has long been a subject of debate. In 1865, one Y. A. Selleck of Wisconsin noted in this copy of the Cemetery Committee's report that the site was outside the burial layout "facing to the northeast." For years the Selleck site was accepted even though it flew in the face of other, less specific, descriptions found in newspaper accounts of the proceedings. In 1973, Dr. Frederick Tilberg, retired Gettysburg park historian, made a compelling case for the site having rested at the spot where the Soldier's Monument now stands. His site replaced Selleck's. In the 1980's the current park historian, Kathy Harrison, offered a third site alternative that seems to match with all the contemporary evidence. Her analysis is based on photographs made of the event. The Harrison site is at the highest point in the area and sits on the present day Brown family plot within the Evergreen Cemetery which adjoins the National cemetery. William Frassanito offered a more definitive analysis of photographs in his 1996 publication, Early Photography at Gettysburg, pp 165-67, wherein he pinpointed the location about 40 yards N.W. of Harrison's Brown plot site.

15. Daniel Skelly, p 26

16. Henry Eyster Jacobs, Gettysburg, 50 Years Ago. THE LUTHERAN, August 7, 1913.

17. Garry Wills, pp 37,38

18. H.C. Holloway, Lincoln at Gettysburg..

19. Ibid

20. Daniel Skelly, p 27

21. Mary Elizabeth Montfort, How a 12 Year Old Girl..

22. Albertus McCreary, A Boy's Experience...

23. Ibid.

24. Liberty Hollinger Glutz, Personal Experiences.. p 14

INDEX